NAVAL FAST STRIKE CRAFT and PATROL BOATS

by

ROY McLEAVY

illustrated by
JOHN W. WOOD
W. HOBSON
J. PELLING
D. SMITH
E. BRUCE

BLANDFORD PRESS
POOLE   DORSET

Blandford Press Ltd
Link House, West Street,
Poole, Dorset BH15 1LL

© Blandford Press 1979
First published 1979

All rights reserved. No part of this book may be reproduced, or transmitted in any form or by any means, electronic or mechanical, including photocopying, recording or by any information storage and retrieval system, without permission in writing from the Publisher.

By the same author

Hovercraft and Hydrofoils

Colour printed by Sackville Press, Billericay
Text set, printed and bound in Great Britain by
Cox & Wyman Ltd,
London, Fakenham and Reading

0 7137 0866 2

FOREWORD

At no time in history have the navies of the world had so varied an assortment of warships and weapons at their disposal. Not only are today's warships more powerful, faster and more seaworthy than in the past, but the weight of their offensive firepower has increased to such an extent that they bear scant resemblance to their predecessors.

Advances in weapon technology have affected warships both large and small. In 1945 a typical motor torpedo-boat displaced 40–50 tons and was armed with one 2-pounder gun, one twin Oerlikon and two torpedo tubes. By comparison its present-day counterpart, a craft like the Combattante III, has a fully laden displacement of 480 tons and is armed with four ship-to-ship missiles, two 21 in. torpedoes, two fully automatic 76 mm. dual-purpose guns and two twin 30 mm. cannon. It packs the 'punch' of a 2,500 ton frigate and can be purchased at only one-sixth of the price.

Because of the immense damage it can inflict on much bigger vessels, a missile-armed fast strike craft is now rated as a major warship.

Unlike the motor torpedo-boats of World War II, which had to move in so close to their targets that they were in constant danger, not only of being blown out of the water by shells, but hit by rifle fire, new generation strike craft, aided by radar, computers, low-light TV cameras and laser range-finders, can unleash their missiles from the horizon by day or night in almost any weather at targets 20 km. away with a 99 per cent. certainty of scoring a hit. Equipped with slightly more sophisticated missiles the strike craft can even engage targets up to 90 km. away, simply by calling on consort vessels or aircraft located nearer to the foe to provide the launched missiles with mid-course guidance. Having launched its missiles, it then depends on its speed, manoeuvrability and electronic counter-measures to escape detection and destruction.

In these days of high inflation and spiralling defence costs the missilecraft is seen by many nations, particularly the smaller ones moving towards economic and military independence, as a 'best buy'. Not only does it meet their immediate strategic and tactical requirements at an attractive price, but its small size and high degree of automation eases the problems of manning and the provision of maintenance and base facilities. In cases, where, because of local sea conditions, additional speed and stability is required, the smaller navies are turning to hydrofoil missilecraft and, in areas where shallows dictate a need to combine speed with amphibious capability, 70 mph hovercraft are available as the missile platform.

Although considerable numbers of fast patrol boats are at present equipped with torpedoes or guns, it should be remembered that many of 25 m. or more in length are capable of being fitted with anti-ship missiles if the need arises.

The pages that follow recount some of the more dramatic events that have taken place in the evolution of both fast strike craft and fast patrol boats, as well as describing the duties they perform, their weapons, their electronic sensors and their propulsion machinery. Full colour illustrations, brief 'character studies' and specifications are provided for the great majority of these vessels in service throughout the world. Since one of the primary objectives of this book is to aid the speedy recognition of these craft, hints on 'spotting' are also included.

Readers finding their interest aroused by this new area of

naval weapons technology and wishing to keep themselves abreast of progress are likely to find themselves busy indeed. A recent survey shows that the fast patrol boat is already the biggest single class of warship in service. Today it accounts for about 60 per cent. of the total number of warships in service and under construction – a share which naval shipbuilders predict will expand annually into the foreseeable future.

Roy McLeavy
Tunbridge Wells
January 1979

ACKNOWLEDGEMENTS

It would have been impossible to have assembled the mass of information contained in this book without the goodwill and co-operation of many members of the shipbuilding and associated industries throughout the world. The author wishes to acknowledge his indebtedness to all the builders of light warships who heeded his pleas for facts and figures and in particular to John Brookes of Vosper Thornycroft, who, before his recent retirement, provided not only information, but also a great deal of advice and encouragement throughout the 'gestation' period.

I am also indebted to my old colleague Ray Blackman, editor of *Jane's Fighting Ships* from 1948 to 1973, to Captain John Moore RN, the current editor of this invaluable publication, as well as to two other well-known warship specialists, Antony Preston, former editor of *Navy International* and Trevor Lenton, editor of *Naval Record*, for filling in a variety of gaps in my knowledge of this field.

Other sources to which acknowledgements are gratefully made are Siegfried Brier and the editors of *Soldat und Technik, Aviation & Marine International, Aviation Week, Sea Power* and *Hovering Craft and Hydrofoil*.

Among the many technical papers referred to in the course of preparing the manuscript were 'Arming the Light Naval Craft' by Cdr Mark Martin RN (Retd), Mark Martin & Partners, Dartmouth; 'General Design Aspects of Small Fast Warships' by A. L. Dorey, Technical Manager, Vosper

Thornycroft (UK) Ltd; 'The Diesel Engine for Powering High Speed Craft' by N. J. Wadley, Senior Marine Applications Engineer, Paxman Diesels Ltd, 'The Amphibious Hovercraft as a Warship' by Ray Wheeler, Technical Director and Chief Designer, British Hovercraft Corporation; 'The Compact Gas-Turbine for Powering Small Fast Ships' by N. J. H. Ballantine, Industrial and Marine Division, Rolls-Royce Ltd; 'Air Defence of Small Fast Warships' by Wg Cdr R. A. G. Ellen, OBE, RAF, British Manufacture and Research Co. Ltd, Grantham and 'Weapon Electronics for Small Fast Warships and Security Vessels' by Capt. Peter Manisty, DSC, RN, Plessey Radar Ltd. All the above were presented at the Symposium on Small Fast Warships and Security Vessels, staged in London in March 1978 by the Royal Institution of Naval Architects.

The author would also like to acknowledge the help and encouragement given by those behind the scenes: Barry Gregory of Blandford Press; Mrs Erika Lock who typed the manuscript; Eugene Kolesnik and Will Horton who worked unstintingly on checking it and finally to Jack Wood and his artists whose colour illustrations depict the new generation of small fast warships with such vivid realism.

THE MINI-WARSHIP – ITS EVOLUTION

Naval history is full of 'David and Goliath' stories in which small lightly built craft have successfully attacked and sunk larger adversaries.

Early equivalents to fast patrol boats were employed by the Phoenicians, Greeks and Romans for interdiction and the penetration of enemy coastal waters and ports. Nearly three hundred years ago fast cutters, mounting light cannon and designed to help enforce and maintain good order at sea, were not uncommon in the Mediterranean, the North Sea and the Baltic. Then in the early 1870s with the advent of the torpedo, came the first major turning point in light warship development. Prompted initially by orders from overseas navies, then by contracts from the British Admiralty, John Isaac Thornycroft, a Thameside boatbuilder, began the construction of specially designed torpedo-boats, based on his series of fast steam launches. They were an immediate success; particularly among the smaller nations and those with limited defence budgets, who recognized it as an inexpensive short-cut to attaining additional power at sea.

Within a decade Thornycroft and Alfred Fernandez Yarrow, another Thames-based boatbuilder were both supplying torpedo-boats by the score to navies throughout the world. Initially these craft had been designed around the spar-type torpedo, a primitive arrangement consisting of an explosive charge on the end of a pole mounted at the bow of the attacking craft. But by the late 1880s this had been replaced by one of a much more formidable variety – an autostabilized, self-propelled torpedo designed in Italy by a gifted English marine engineer, Robert Whitehead. Fired by pressurized steam from a long tube located at either the bow or stern of the boat, the Whitehead Torpedo Mk III, built in 1876, was 35.6 cm. (14 in.) in diameter, travelled underwater at 21 knots, had a range of 550 m. (600 yds) and carried 26.3 kg. (58 lb) of gun cotton. By the mid-1890s, the names of Whitehead and Thornycroft had become synonymous with that of the motor torpedo-boat and were to remain so for three-quarters of a century.

Not surprisingly, before long some of the customers for the early lightly built craft began to recognize their severe shortcomings in open sea conditions. They decided they wanted bigger, more seaworthy craft with increased firepower, greater speed and longer range. New designs were prepared which came within three categories. Those of about 60 ft in length and designed for hoisting aboard battleships and cruisers were known as Second Class; craft of around 125 ft were known as First Class; and those with a length in excess of 145 ft were classified as Seagoing.

As the attention of overseas navies began to focus on the larger craft, so the British Admiralty decided that the time had come to introduce a counterpart – the torpedo-boat destroyer (TBD), a term later abbreviated to destroyer. More than thirty TBDs had been ordered by 1893 and in 1895 the Royal Navy proudly demonstrated the performance capability of its new class of warship to the world by setting up a new international sea speed record of 29.3 knots with the Boxer, one of the first of the new breed, built by Thornycroft-Laird. A typical TBD displaced about 240 tons and in addition to its main armament of three torpedo tubes, mounted one 12-pounder and three 6-pounders. It was soon recognized that in practice the TBD had all the qualities of a super torpedo-boat. Here was a true case of the remedy proving worse than the disease. Not only was it capable of

TYPICAL SOVIET LIGHT AA MOUNTINGS

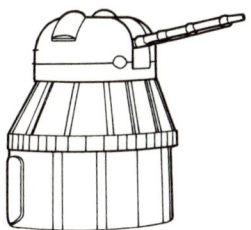

L/65 fully-automatic remote-controlled twin 30 mm. gun mounting. Rate of fire, about 500 rounds/minute/barrel. Range 3–4,000 m.

Twin 25 mm. Semi-enclosed mounting employed on a number of older Soviet fast patrol boats and coastal minesweepers.

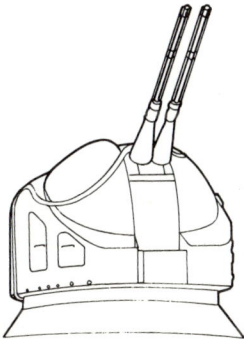

Fully enclosed automatic twin 57 mm. AA mounting fitted to the Turya, Nanushka and frigates and destroyers.

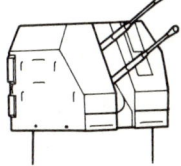

Enclosed 25 mm. naval mounting. May be remotely controlled.

outstripping and destroying small torpedo-boats because of its vastly superior speed, seaworthiness, range and firepower but it was also capable of attacking cruisers and battleships both inshore and in open seas.

The motor torpedo-boat was the first light naval craft in modern naval history to have its own weapon, its own identity and a recognized offensive role. MTBs, as they became known, were employed extensively by the opposing sides in both World Wars. Readers wishing to learn more about the design of these craft and the tactics employed by their commanders should refer to the many excellent books on the subject.

In the years immediately following World War II there was a marked lack of interest in MTBs, although small numbers were built for navies of the newly emergent nations and a few of the older ones, including Denmark, Greece, Norway and Sweden, which required them to defend their deeply scored, fretted and broken coasts, a task for which the torpedo-boat is ideal.

Then in 1967 came an event which projected the light craft from torpedo-boat and a range of lesser roles to that of major warship. On 21 October 1967, Russian-built 'Styx' anti-ship missiles fired by a Komar-class missile craft within Port Said Harbour sank the Israeli destroyer Eilat at a range of ten miles. Russia's drive to surpass the United States in gun power had led them to start experimenting with anti-ship missiles in the early 1950s. Unable to match American seaborne air power, they developed this weapon to enable small converted torpedo-boats to threaten any US Navy carriers approaching Soviet-occupied territory.

Anti-ship missiles have given today's fast patrol boats firepower out of all proportion to their size. They can inflict severe damage on much larger ships while still retaining sufficient speed and manoeuvrability to escape detection before completing their attacks and making their escape. The pairing of the fast patrol boat with the anti-ship missile has had an impact as dramatic on naval planning as the introduction of the submarine in World War I and naval aviation and aircraft carriers in the 1920s and 1930s. Naval historians compare the sinking of the Eilat with the battle between the first Ironclads during the American Civil War and General Billy Mitchell's early demonstration of the effect of air power on battleships.

Patrol craft – some little more than motorboats with a limited weapon capability – are generally small vessels, employed not only for naval duties but also for customs, coastguard, police and immigration authority work. Although many carry light armament they are not really considered to be fighting ships. Built to a wide range of designs and varying considerably in terms of electronic navigation and surveillance equipment they range in length from about 12 to 35 m.

Fast strike (or attack) craft are considered to range in displacement from between 100 to 400 tonnes. The armament of the average strike craft includes anti-ship missiles in their launching canisters, automatic dual-purpose guns for use against sea and air targets and rapid-fire cannon plus, occasionally, surface-to-air missiles for close-in self-defence against low-flying aircraft or anti-ship missiles. Speeds of above 40 knots are not normally required and this level of performance generally can be supplied by diesel engines. Most FPBs today are powered by either two diesels driving two propeller shafts or four diesels, driving four shafts. Where higher performance is necessary gas-turbines are normally fitted, but it is exceptional for a missilecraft to exceed 50 knots since the attainment of this speed requires not only gas-turbine power but also the fitting of super-cavitating propellers.

Higher speeds still are attainable by employing hovercraft and hydrofoils as missile platforms. Apart from its speed advantages the amphibious capabilities of the fully skirted hovercraft enables it to make the transition from sea to shore without difficulty, permitting it to operate in shallow water and even across mud flats, marshes and sand banks. It is equally at home on seas frequently frozen over in winter, like the Baltic, enjoying full mobility when all other surface craft are brought to a standstill for several months. Fast strike hovercraft can be deployed from hides above the shoreline and 'scrambled' to intercept and interrogate approaching suspect craft, or alternatively, they can be controlled from a mobile base, like a 'mother' ship patrolling off-shore. A further quality of the missile-carrying amphibious hovercraft is that because of its very low acoustic and magnetic underwater signatures it is virtually immune to underwater explosions.

From the point of view of cost/effectiveness the 50–60-knot hydrofoil is also an attractive investment. It costs far less than the destroyer or frigate it replaces and besides being much faster, a craft with electronically controlled fully submerged foils reduces its speed only slightly in higher sea states. In fact, it is now generally accepted that a hydrofoil is the only type of escort vessel which can either match or exceed the seaway performance of the main vessels of a task force. Additional advantages are its ability to provide a very steady platform for its weapons and for launching and taking aboard a helicopter in rough weather, plus, of course, the improved economics which can be realized with the introduction of high speeds. Since the hydrofoil patrol craft will probably average three times the speed of the vessel it replaces it will be capable of patrolling an area three times the size, allowing a proportional reduction in the number of patrol craft required to undertake a particular task.

Other points in its favour are that it has greater manoeuvrability, its maintenance requirements are generally lower than those of comparable conventional vessels, and its crewing requirements are lower. The reduced maintenance is due very largely to the exceptionally smooth riding qualities of the latest military hydrofoils and their relatively low pitch and roll angles. On conventional patrol boats of the planing hull type accelerations of 10 g have been recorded – but crews have not been able to tolerate this for long. An average person finds that accelerations are perceptible at .01 g, start becoming uncomfortable at about 0.1 g and become intolerable over extended periods at 1 g. U.S. Navy crews operating Boeing's PHM patrol hydrofoil missilecraft in the Mediterranean expect to find vertical acceleration remaining below 0.1 g at a speed of 45 knots for more than 95 per cent. of the time, while those operating in the Baltic will find them below 0.1 g for 90 per cent. of the time.

Navies naturally rely on their fast strike craft for a quick response in an emergency, and, therefore, one of the primary requirements is that they should be capable of sailing at high speed. Hydrofoils and hovercraft offer higher speeds than those attainable by fast strike craft and fast patrol boats with conventional displacement hulls, consequently the demand for these newer, non-displacement craft will almost certainly continue to grow. A clear indication of this trend is that, at the time of writing, thirteen navies have hydrofoils on order or in service while another seven have either ordered or are about to order hovercraft.

Now for a word or two about small warships in general – how they are built, the machinery that sets them in motion, their weapons and electronics.

Hulls

The modern fast strike craft is a direct descendant of the destroyers and motor torpedo-boats of World War II. In some cases present-day hulls bear many of the characteristics of their forebears, in other cases they differ quite considerably. The British tradition of the hard-chine, planing type hull, popular with most Allied torpedo-boat builders during the war years has now been discarded in favour of a round bilge type hull with a knuckle forward to deflect spray, increase buoyancy at the bow and dampen pitch in heavy seas. Hard chines were introduced as a means of safeguarding lateral stability on planing hull designs but at the speeds required of today's craft, the high accelerations generated by this hull form in rough water would result in intensive heaving and slamming which would not only prove unacceptable to the crew but would damage the sensitive weaponry and its associated electronics.

The round bilge light craft was introduced in Germany and was used extensively by Lürssen Werft for their wartime S-boats. Because of its improved seakeeping it has also been adopted in recent years by French, Swedish, Norwegian and Israeli shipyards. In fact most of the world's small fast warships now employ this form of construction.

The structural design of the small warship does not differ fundamentally from that of any other small craft. A typical main hull structure is of welded steel and is built on the longitudinal system with web frames and longitudinal stiffening members. Considerable care has to be taken in the design to keep weight to a minimum in the interest of performance, but rather heavier plating and additional framing is employed in the forward section of the hull to withstand wave impacts experienced when encountering seas at high speed. The upper deck and superstructure are constructed in partly welded and partly riveted marine grade aluminium alloy. Because of its light weight and reduced maintenance requirements, the use of aluminium in small hulls is likely to be increased to include decks and main structural bulkheads.

Mild steel is one of the most popular materials with shipbuilders because it is not expensive; it is easily fabricated by welding and is strong for its weight. However, patrol boats have been built successfully in timber, aluminium and reinforced plastic or a combination of these materials. Timber, once used widely for small craft has one very big disadvantage – it is prone to rot. Another disadvantage is that although at one time a cheap material for boatbuilding, timber is now very expensive, and for these reasons vessels of timber construction are likely to become rarer in future.

Ship length and displacement is dictated mainly by the extent of the armament it is required to carry. Once the customer has selected the weapons fit, the length of the ship can be determined from the amount of space required for the various guns, surface-to-surface missiles and their associated electronics. Most anti-ship missiles can only be fired within certain limits of roll and pitch and vertical accelerations. Active or roll damping fins are fitted to some craft to reduce or dampen the overall roll motion and thereby improve the seakeeping characteristics of these designs, particularly at high speed. Roll reduction factors of between 50 per cent. and 80 per cent. are being achieved consistently with these fins or 'stabilizers', and in view of the necessity for the craft to offer as stable a platform as possible when preparing to launch its missiles, their use is likely to become more widespread in the years immediately ahead.

Power Plant

With the introduction of lightweight, high-speed marine diesels and gas-turbines, the petrol engine, employed extensively on World War II motor torpedo-boats, has almost completely disappeared. It is of interest to note that during 1939–1945 the great majority of Allied MTBs were powered by petrol engines of about 1,000 hp per shaft, and to extend their range deck-mounted long-range tanks had to be fitted. During the same period the S-boats of the German Navy were using diesel engines developing up to 2,000–2,500 hp per shaft.

There is little doubt that there is a marked preference in navies today for high speed diesel engines, which are available in a power range of up to 6,000 hp per shaft. Their main advantages are their economy and reliability, combined with the fact that a diesel-powered craft is less expensive to purchase, its fuel costs and maintenance overheads are lower and trained diesel engineers are more readily available for repair and overhaul. Considering that the high speed diesel can attain 8–12,000 hours between overhaul the maintenance cost is less than half that of a comparable marinized gas-turbine. For economical cruising the engine will operate for long periods at low speeds and remain capable of delivering full power on immediate call. Diesels can also deliver full power continuously for several days, although this obviously reduces the normal time allowed between maintenance periods. However, when a substantial increase in power is required the specific weight of the diesel engine becomes prohibitive and, for larger vessels, the employment of gas-turbines is essential.

In addition, for large conventional FPBs, hydrofoils and hovercraft of larger tonnage, gas-turbines do offer substantial advantages. They develop more power per unit of space and weight, are easier to produce, provide very high torque at low rotational speeds, warm up and accelerate more rapidly and, finally, they are available in a selection of powers in combination of one to four engines from 1,000–192,000 shp. Marinized gas-turbines are adapted from existing aircraft power plants – that for the Boeing/NATO PHM is developed from the General Electric TF39 which powers the C-5A transport and the DC-10 Trijet – combined with specially designed free-power turbines which convert the gas energy to rotative mechanical power. The rotor of the turbine is free to turn independently of the gas generator's speed, and can, therefore, supply variable horse-power output and rotational speeds. Since the gas-turbines were not designed for service in a marine environment, the turbine blades are coated against salt water ingestion and magnesium parts have been replaced with a superior resistance to salt water corrosion. Special filters are fitted to the mouth of the gas-turbine air intake to prevent salt water from reaching the turbine's blades.

Where a long-range cruise requirement exists for gas-turbine powered fast patrol boats, a CODAG (Combined Diesel and Gas-turbine) arrangement can be used. A typical system would be a four-shaft system employing twin Proteus gas-turbines each driving a fixed-pitch or controllable-pitch propeller via an inner vee-drive gearbox and shaft and two diesels, both driving controllable-pitch propellers via two outer inclined shafts. A typical sprint speed employing gas-turbine power would be in the region of 38–40 knots while the cruising speed with the diesels alone would be about 25–28 knots. Rolls-Royce has installed the Proteus in single, double and triple arrangements in a combination of propulsion forms of CODAG, COGAG and CODOG.

Weapons

A typical weapons fit for a modern strike craft of 300–400 tons displacement comprises a medium calibre automatic gun for use against other ships, shore bombardment and anti-aircraft fire; a medium calibre automatic cannon of 20, 30, 35 or 40 mm., for close-in AA defence and use against surface targets, and a surface-to-surface missile system with two to six missile launchers/containers, each with a self-contained active or semi-active homing missile. Providing stowage space is available spare rounds may be carried also. The launcher/container serves as a packing case for transporting the missile to the ship and protects it from the weather when at sea. It permits the missile to be delivered to a vessel as a complete and tested item and once it has been attached to the permanent deck mounts on the ship it is ready for immediate firing. Once it has been plugged-in, testing can be undertaken automatically from the missile control panel in the ship's combat information centre (CIC).

Among the more sophisticated anti-ship missiles entering service with the Western navies is the McDonnell Douglas Harpoon, which has been ordered so far by a dozen or more nations. The Harpoon is in fact the U.S. Navy's main high-subsonic anti-ship tactical cruise missile and has been designed for launching from all classes of U.S. Navy ships apart from patrol gunboats.

Pencil-thin, it is 4.57 m. long, with four controllable aerodynamic fins which guide its course while in flight. It is fired from a quadruple launcher, designed initially for installation aboard the Boeing PHM, but which is now in use on many other small fast patrol boats. On firing, a solid propellant boost motor propels the Harpoon on a ballistic trajectory until the booster separates from the main body. Power from a small turbojet then takes over and the missile descends to a substantially lower cruising height, determined by a radar altimeter, and virtually skims the wave tops. In the terminal phase of the attack the Harpoon performs a rapid climb to elude or confuse close-in automatic cannon fire then dives on to its quarry, a manoeuvre which enhances the effectiveness of its warhead.

Target data from the ship's electronic surveillance system is supplied to the missile via a data processor, a small digital computer, which receives data concerning the target from the vessel's own search and surveillance radar systems, or in the case of targets beyond the horizon, from other ships or aircraft. From the information and plots provided, the computer then programmes the missile in readiness for launching. Once launched from its canister no further data inputs are provided by the ship. Course correction is supplied by a miniaturized vertical guidance system, comprising an altitude reference system and a digital computer. Its altitude as it heads towards its target is constantly checked by a radar altimeter and corrections are made via electromechanical activators altering the incidence of the fins. Guidance to the target in the final stage of the attack – the 'terminal phase' as it is known – is provided by an active homing radar system, a sensing device, which locks on to the target until the missile finally strikes home.

One of the more awesome aspects of the Harpoon, which carries a warhead packed with penetrating blast-type high explosive, is its ability to overcome both electronic jamming and attempts by the target to take evasive action in the terminal phase of the attack. If its radar senses attempts at jamming, it simply switches automatically to another frequency and its high degree of manoeuvrability enables it to cope with any efforts by the target to evade it on its approach. Details of the anti-ship missiles employed by most strike craft is given in Table I.

Electronics

Future duels between fast strike craft of 300–400 tons will almost certainly be won by the boat with the best electronics. The weapons systems of all craft of this type are controlled by electronics but some systems are more comprehensive, more sensitive and have much faster reaction times than others.

The commander of a fast strike craft has to have at his finger tips the latest information available, not only concerning changes in the local tactical situation at sea, but also the situation regarding hostile aircraft. Because of the sheer volume of the information input, manual processing would take far too long to be of practical use. Only by the introduction of an electronic data processing system is it possible for him to be presented with an almost automatic flow of data.

For this reason fire control and action information organization systems (AIOs) have been developed for small fast craft. At one time these systems were so large that they could only be installed on cruisers and destroyers. But microminiaturization and the employment of integrated circuits have permitted the construction of much smaller computers. In fact today, because of their small size computers and their associated displays are often incorporated in the same consoles.

Typical of contemporary integrated command and control

systems is ACIS (Automatic Combat Information System), employed on the Type 143 craft operated by the West German Navy. This comprises surveillance radar, a computer, display unit, data transmission unit and a fire control system for its two guns, four Exocet missiles and torpedoes. The radar is employed for both surface and air surveillance, IFF (Identification Friend or Foe), directing weapons and navigation. At the heart of the system is the computer which functions as the central control point, collecting the information supplied, evaluating it and feeding it to the display of the fire control system and into the data transmission system.

The commander decides what action to take according to the information available on the tactical display. If in doubt, he can confer with other commanders in the flotilla via a data link. The data transfer system provides a direct automatic information exchange not only with other units in the flotilla, but also with land bases, so that flotilla commanders can receive immediate target assignment instructions from a central naval operations headquarters.

As a rule fire control systems are designed to control one or more guns against either the same or different aircraft or surface targets and to engage simultaneously if necessary, several surface targets.

Additional equipment carried aboard the Type 143 includes HF and VHF transmitters/receivers, a radio-teleprinter, a horizontally stabilized gyrocompass, an echo sounder, a distance measuring log and a Decca navigator.

Gunfire control is initiated by a system which employs optical or electro-optical tracking and is equipped to operate either one or two main gun mountings. This is the optronic director, an instrument which combines four kinds of sensor: binoculars, a laser rangefinder, a day and night low-light television and a thermal imaging projector for use at night or in conditions of poor visibility. The laser rangefinder gives precise ranging. The optronic director is guided straight to the bearing of the target by information from the surveillance radar which is fed to it via a computer linked to the fire control console.

Once the operator handling the optronic director begins to track the target, the gunfire control computer trains the guns and waits for the target to come within firing range. Immediately it comes within range an X-band tracking radar takes over and feeds the gunfire control computer with all the necessary data to engage the target or targets automatically. Modern tracking radar is capable of detecting and tracking a strike aircraft at a distance of 20–25 km. and a sea-skimming type anti-ship missile homing-in at a height of 3 m. at a distance of 12–15 km. The equipment can be fitted to almost any fast strike and patrol craft with an overall length of 40 m. or more.

Most craft are equipped with an automatic classification ESM (electronic warfare support measures) set, which is installed for missile warning and the over-the-horizon targeting of every surface unit. Radar warning receivers are fitted to alert the ship's crew when the craft is illuminated by hostile radar; infrared and electronic jammers are installed to disrupt the electronics of any weapon employing an infrared sensor to 'hunt' the vessel. In addition to powerful ESM jammers, chaff and flare rockets are generally carried by small craft as a means of screening themselves against a missile's radar and infrared homing systems. Table 2 provides the names of many of the major companies supplying weapons and electronics for strike and patrol craft; Table 3 lists some of the most widely used Gunfire Control Systems and Table 4 lists four typical search radars employed on small warships.

Guns

Various light, small calibre rapid-firing naval gun mounts are available for use on fast patrol craft as dual-purpose anti-aircraft and anti-ship systems. Among the most widely used of these are the Oto Melara 76/62 Compact; the Bofors 57 mm. L/70 and single 120 mm. dual-purpose mount;

Components of the Otomat
anti-ship missile system.

1. Homing head
2. Gyro platform
3. Junction box
4. Flight computer
5. Fuel tank
6. Sustainer
7. Warhead
8. Altimeter
9. Autopilot
10. Converter
11. Oil tank
12. Fin actuators

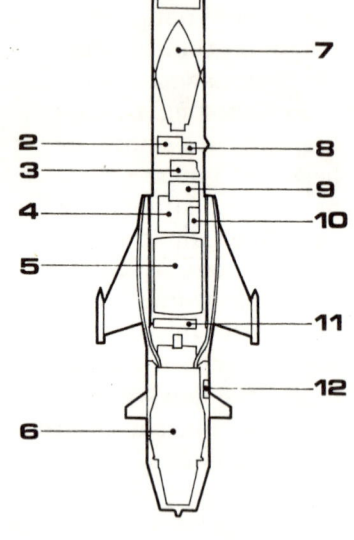

Typical weapon electronics fit on a 50 m. fast strike craft with guns, missiles and an optional helicopter. *With acknowledgements to Plessey Radar Limited.*

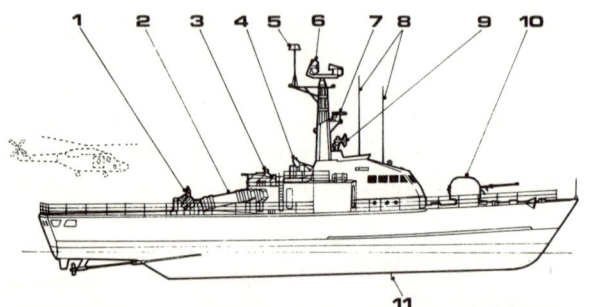

1. Chaff launchers. 2. Ship/ship missile. 3. Short range gun.
4. Electro optical tracker. 5. ESM. 6. Surveillance radar.
7. Navigation radar. 8. Whip aerials. 9. Tracking radar.
10. Medium range gun. 11. Log.

Oerlikon's 30 and 35 mm. twin mounts and the twin 30 mm. Emerlec-30. Most make extensive use of light alloys and glass reinforced plastics in their construction in the interests of cost and weight saving. All can be switched to remote control when necessary and can be brought into action unmanned from the weapon console of the vessel's fire control system until all on-mounting rounds have been fired. The Bofors 57 mm. L/70, arming Sweden's Spicas for example, is in a plastic cupola and has a rate of fire of 200 rounds per minute. The first 40 rounds, considered sufficient to engage two or three aircraft, can be fired automatically without the aid of the crew. Two different types of round are used with this gun, the first a proximity-fused, prefragmented shell designed for use against approaching anti-ship missiles, manned aircraft and RPVs, and the second, an anti-ship shell with more than the usual amount of high explosive in its warhead. Equipped with a short-delay fuse so that it explodes within the ship, this penetrating type of shell is said by experts to be two to three times more effective than earlier types. Test firings under sea conditions have shown that when using Bofors 57 mm. proximity fuse ammunition against towed targets a salvo of two or three rounds normally destroys the target at a range of 2–3 km., even when it is engaged in sea state 4.

Apart from its main medium calibre guns for use against surface, shore and air targets, a large modern strike craft is also likely to mount at least one small calibre gun of 20, 30, 35 or 40 mm. for close-in, anti-aircraft defence and skirmishes with lighter craft. Additionally small arms are likely to be provided for boarding and shore parties. Table 5 lists the characteristics of three widely used gun mounts.

Spotting them at Sea

At first glance all fast strike craft and patrol boats tend to look very much alike. Careful study however, will quickly show that each type differs quite remarkably from the next, not just in one prominent feature, but generally in a number of points, large and small. Each, in brief, has its own distinctive characteristics. Study the hull shape closely and see how the craft 'sits' on the water; study the lines of the bridge and the deckhouse superstructure. Note the length of the deckhouse and see whether it is set well forward on the hull, at the centre, or well back. Compare the Spica in this respect with the Osa and the Nasty with the P.6. Pay attention to the type of armament carried and its location. A little concentration will soon reveal the differences between the Bofors, Oto Melaras, Oerlikons and Emerlecs – not to mention the weapons used by the strike and patrol craft of the Warsaw Pact countries. Pick out which designs carry torpedo tubes on their decks and the positions of the light guns installed for close-in defence against missiles and low-flying aircraft. Finally, don't overlook two other important aids for craft identity – the masts supporting the surveillance, tracking and navigation radar and the size, shape and location of the air intakes and exhausts of gas-turbine powered craft.

All learning is based on repetition. For readers who feel a mnemonic might help to check through the salient features of each craft, try SHEEW – Superstructure, Hull, Engines, Electronics (aerial and scanner array) and Weapons. Watch out for modifications, too. Masts may be modified from time to time, types of guns may be changed and the torpedo-tubes or missile launchers may not always be carried. You may well find your attempts to memorize the characteristics of these craft are more fun and less obviously analytical if you try one or more of the following methods:

- copying the side elevations freehand on graph paper
- tracing or copying photographs
- starting a scrap collection of photos from newspapers, magazines and naval journals

– making simple waterline models in balsa.
– producing three-dimensional silhouette models in thin card.

Remember practice makes perfect, and whether you practise your spotting under the excitement and stress of operational conditions or in a purely leisurely way on vacation, it is hoped that many will find in the pages that follow the help they need in distinguishing friend from foe.

Fast Attack Craft Classification

The nomenclature employed in Europe and the United States for patrol and attack craft differs considerably.
EUROPE: In general, the term Fast Patrol Boat (FPB) is applied only to craft employed primarily for coastal patrol and armed with light weapons only. Fast Attack Craft, also frequently referred to as 'strike' craft, are classified by the weapons they carry. FAC(M) denotes Fast Attack Craft – Missile; FAC(T), Fast Attack Craft – Torpedo; and FAC(G), Fast Attack Craft – Gun. Should the craft be of non-displacement type – either a hovercraft or hydrofoil – this information is carried at the end of the classification. However, it should be remembered that a number of fast attack craft combine missiles with torpedoes and some can be converted from one role to another overnight to suit the tactical situation. In addition some are equipped for minelaying and ASW roles.
UNITED STATES: The classifications currently in use are the following: Coastal Patrol Boat, CPC; Coastal Patrol and Interdiction Craft, CPIC; Patrol Boat, PB; Patrol Craft (Fast), PCF; Patrol Gunboat Hydrofoil, PGH; Patrol Combatant Missile (Hydrofoil), PCM(H); Fast Patrol Craft, PTF.

Table I – TYPICAL SURFACE-TO-SURFACE MISSILES EMPLOYED ON FAST STRIKE CRAFT

Country, Manufacturer and System	Maximum Range	Speed	Warhead Weight	Power Plant	Guidance Method
France					
Aerospatiale Exocet MM38	42 km.	Mach 0.93	150–200 kg.	Two stage solid fuel rocket	Inertial cruise and terminal active radar
Exocet MM40	70 km.	Mach 0.93	28.4 kg.	Two stage solid fuel rocket	Inertial cruise and terminal active radar
Aerospatiale SS11	2 n. miles	330 knots	28.4 kg.	Two stage solid fuel rocket	Wire guided, optical tracking
Aerospatiale SS12	4.4 n. miles	—	28.4 kg.	Two stage solid fuel rocket	Wire guided, optical tracking
France/Italy					
Oto Melara/Matra Otomat	60–180 km.	Mach 0.9	210 kg.	Turbomeca Turbojet	Inertial cruise and terminal radar
Israel					
Gabriel I	14 n. miles	Mach 0.7	180 kg.	Two stage solid fuel rocket	Radar and terminal active radar plus optical/radio command in interference
Gabriel II	26 n. miles	Mach 0.7	180 kg.	Two stage solid fuel rocket	Radar and terminal active radar plus optical/radio command in interference
Italy					
Sistel SpA Sea Killer I (Nettuno)	6 n. miles plus	Mach 1.9	77 lb	Single stage solid fuel rocket	Beam-rider plus radio or optical command
Sea Killer II (Vulcano)	13 n. miles	Mach 1.9	155 lb	Two stage solid fuel rocket	Beam-rider plus radio or optical command

Norway
Kongsberg Vaapenfabrik

Penguin I	27 km.	Mach 0.7	264 lb	Two stage solid fuel rocket	Inertial and passive infra-red
Penguin II				Two stage solid fuel rocket	Inertial and passive infra-red

U.S.S.R.

SS-N-2 Codename 'Styx'	23 n. miles	Mach 0.7		Two stage solid fuel rocket	Radar – Infra-red or radar homing
SS-N-9	150 n. miles	In excess of Mach 1	HE or nuclear	Solid fuel rocket	Autopilot command plus IR or radar homing. Likely to have provision for external or mid-course guidance by fixed-wing aircraft or helicopter.

U.S.A.
McDonnell Douglas

Harpoon	50 n. miles	Mach 0.9	400 lb +	Solid fuel launcher. Turbojet cruise	Pre-programmed inertial, plus terminal active radar.

Table 2 – PRODUCTS OF LEADING COMPANIES

Company	Products
PEAB—Philips Elektronikindustrier	Search radars, 9LV Series Fire Control Systems, Tactical Display Systems, Philax Chaff Systems.
SATT	Active and Passive Electronic Warfare Systems and Chaff Systems.
Bofors AB Kongsberg Vapenfabrik	57 mm., 40 mm. Gun Mounts, As Rocket Launchers. PENGUIN SS Missile System, Bofors Guns, MSI-80' Fire Control Systems
Decca Company	Navigation Radar, RDL Series of Electronic Warfare Systems and Data Display Systems.
Ferranti DSD	CAAIS Data Display Systems, GSA Series of Fire Control Systems.
GEC-Marconi	Search Radars, Sapphire Fire Control System, NCS Stable Datum System.
Plessey Radar	AWS Series of Search Radar, Data Display Systems.
Sperry Gyroscope	Sea Archer Fire Control System, Stable Datum Systems, Sapphire Fire Control System. (With Marconi).
B-MARC-Oerlikon	30 mm. and 20 mm. Gun Mounts.
MEL Co	Electronic Warfare Equipment (SUSIE), Protean Chaff System.
LSE—Laurence Scott	Optical Fire Control Systems.
Contraves and Sistel	Search Radar, Sea Hunter Fire Control Systems, Sea Killer Missile System.
Oerlikon	20 mm., 30 mm. & 35 mm. Gun Mounts.
Elettronica	Active and Passive Electronic Warfare Systems.
OTO Melara	OTOMAT SS Missile System (With Matra, France), 35 mm. and 76 mm. Gun Mounts.
Breda	40 mm. Gun Mounts, Chaff Launcher.
Selenia	Search Radars, Data Display Systems, Fire Control Radar, Active and Passive Electronic Warfare Systems.
ELSAG	Gun and Missile Fire Control Systems. (ARGO Series, DARDO System).

SMA	Search Radars, Radar Homing Heads.
Officine Galilileo	Fire Control Systems.
Hollandse Signaalapparaten	Gun and Missile Fire Control Systems (M 20 and M 40 Series), Search Radars, Data Display Systems, Electronic Warfare Systems.
Aérospatiale—SNIAS	EXOCET SS Missile System Radar Homing Heads.
Electronic Marcel	
Dassault	
Thomson CSF	Search Radars, CASTOR Series of Fire Control Systems, Data Display Systems, Electronic Warfare Systems.
CIT Alcatel	As Equipment. 30 mm. Gun Mounts.
SAMM	
Engins Matra	OTOMAT SS Missile System. (With OTO Melara)

Table 3 – GUN FIRE CONTROL SYSTEMS

Manufacturer and System	Tracking Method and Frequency	Approximate Detection and Tracking Range km.	Approximate Weight kg.
Hollandse Signaalapparat[n] WM 20 Series	Monopulse I Band Radar + Optional Optronic	30 25	2800 (Including search Radar)
ELSAG ARGO NA 10 Series	Conical Scan I Band Radar and TV	30 25	1100
Thomson CSF CASTOR 2	Monopulse I Band Radar	30 25	1750
Marconi-Sperry Sapphire	Monopulse I Band Radar + TV	30 25	1825
Sperry Sea Archer	Optical + Radar or Laser ranging	8 3	700
Ferranti GSA Gunsight	Optical (For small cal guns)	5 2	8

By courtesy of Mark Martin & Partners

Table 4 – SEARCH RADARS

Manufacturer and Type	Frequency and Data Rate	Detection Range Small Aircraft km.	Approximate Weight kg. whether Stabilized Antenna
Thomson CSF TRITON	G Band 24 rpm	35	1020 Unstabilized
Hollandse Signaalapparat[n] M 20 Series	I Band 60 rpm	30	2800 Stabilized and also includes Fire Control System
Selenia—SMA RAN 11 L-X	D & I Bands 30/15 rpm	35	1000 Stabilized
Plessey AWS 4	E/F Band 20 rpm	40	1400 Unstabilized

By courtesy of Mark Martin & Partners

Table 5 – GUN MOUNTS

	OTO Melara Compact 76/62 76 mm.	BREDA-BOFORS Compact Twin 40 mm.	OERLIKON Twin Naval Mount GCM 30 mm.
Gun and Calibre			
Rate of Fire RPM	85	600	1,300
Projectile Weight	6.3 kg.	0.96-0.88 kg.	0.36 kg.
Ready to Fire Rounds	80	444 or 736	320
Effective Range	SU Abt 12 km. AA Abt 5 km.	SU Abt 4 km. AA Abt 2.5 km.	SU Abt 3 km. AA Abt 1.5 km.
Weight with Ammunition	8850 kg.	6000 or 7000 kg.	2020 kg.
Swept Radius	5.2 metres	3.0 metres	2.5 metres
Power Required	440 v 60 hz 50 kva	440 v 60 hz 14 kva	440 v 60 hz 10 kva

By courtesy of Mark Martin & Partners

1
ASHEVILLE CLASS

PG100 Douglas, an Asheville class patrol combatant (PG) built for the US Navy. Powered by a 13,300shp GE LM1500 gas-turbine for 'sprint' performance and twin 1,450hp diesels for cruising, it can attain a speed of 40 knots within one minute of full stop in the lower sea states.

Inset: Outboard profile showing one of the mounting arrangements for the standard anti-ship missile.

2
AL FULK
Al Fulk, one of a class of seven fast patrol boats built in the mid-1970s by Brooke Marine for the Sultanate of Oman. During 1977, the first three in the class, Al Bushra, Al Mansur and Al Nejah, were rearmed with a twin MM38 Exocet launcher aft.

MADARAKA CLASS
Jamhuri, a 145 ton patrol boat of the Madaraka class operated by the Kenyan Navy. Built by Brooke Marine, it is powered by two Paxman Valenta diesels which provide the craft with a top speed of about 26 knots.

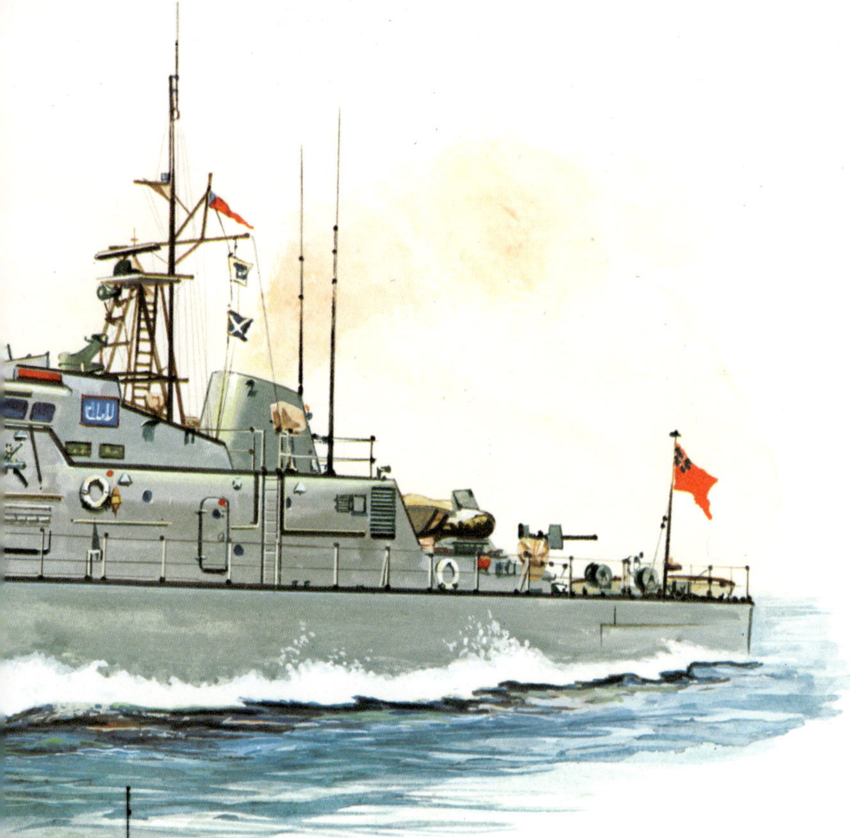

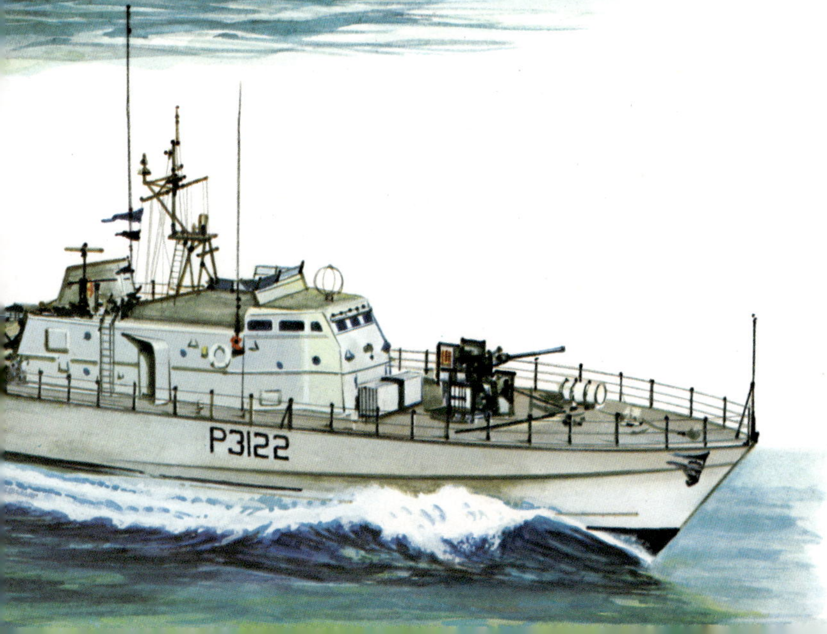
P3122

3
Astrapi, transferred to the Hellenic Navy in 1967, is powered by three Rolls-Royce Proteus gas-turbines and has a top speed of about 55 knots. Its main armament is four 21in. (533mm.) torpedoes.

4
AZTECA CLASS

The Mexican Navy's Azteca class was designed in the United Kingdom to meet a requirement for a fast patrol boat capable of continuous operation in rough waters off Mexico's Atlantic and Pacific seaboards and a speed of 25 knots. Twenty-one of these 34m. fishery protection and coastguard craft have been supplied by Scottish shipyards and ten more are under construction in Mexico, where there are plans to build a further fifty, some of which will be exported.

5
BH.7 WELLINGTON CLASS

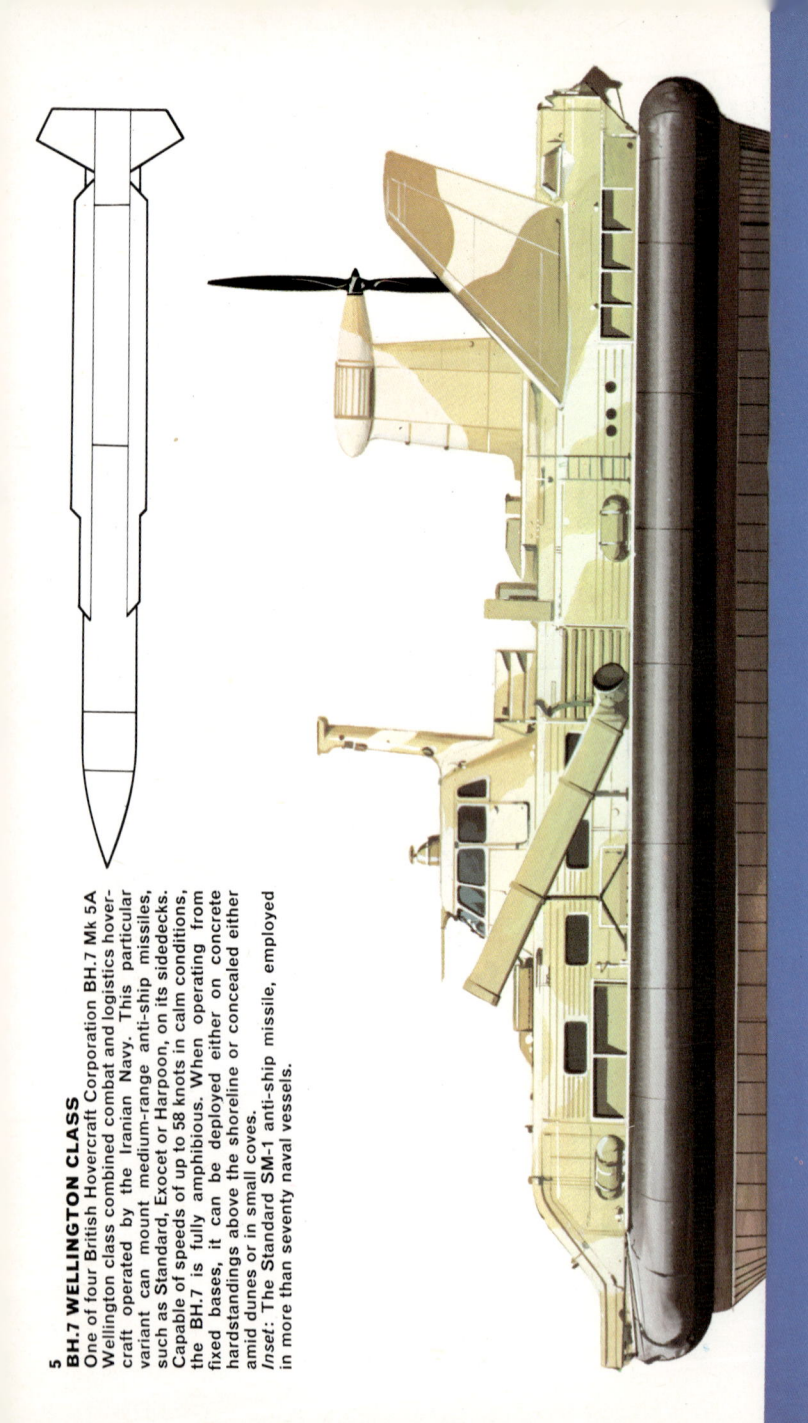

One of four British Hovercraft Corporation BH.7 Mk 5A Wellington class combined combat and logistics hovercraft operated by the Iranian Navy. This particular variant can mount medium-range anti-ship missiles, such as Standard, Exocet or Harpoon, on its sidedecks. Capable of speeds of up to 58 knots in calm conditions, the BH.7 is fully amphibious. When operating from fixed bases, it can be deployed either on concrete hardstandings above the shoreline or concealed either amid dunes or in small coves.

Inset: The Standard SM-1 anti-ship missile, employed in more than seventy naval vessels.

BABOCHKA CLASS
Babochka (Butterfly) is the latest and largest hydrofoil patrol craft to enter service with the Soviet Navy. Powered by three large gas-turbines, each delivering about 25,000shp, it has been designed for anti-submarine warfare and has a top speed in excess of 50 knots. A triple trainable ASW torpedo mount can be installed on the forward deck between the deckhouse and the twin 30mm. L/65 automatic anti-aircraft mounting. Exhaust discharge to atmosphere is via three angled funnels on the aft deck.

7
CPIC
One of the novelties of the US Navy's CPIC (Coastal Patrol Interdiction Craft) is the employment of waterjet propulsion, enabling it to operate closer inshore than other craft of similar displacement. Another key feature is its Honeywell radar gunfire control system, designed to train the two twin 30mm. Emerlec gun mounts on other surface craft and spotter aircraft.

Inset: An Emerlec-30 twin 30mm. gun mount, for anti-missile, anti-aircraft and surface action.

COMBATTANTE II CLASS

Left: Combattante II, the first class of missile strike craft to be designed and built by Western nations to counter the Styx-equipped Komas and Osas built by the Soviet Union. The first batch of twelve were built by Constructions Mécaniques de Normandie (CMN) to a Lürssen design and supplied to the Israeli Navy between 1965-69 as its Saar class.

COMBATTANTE III CLASS

Below: Latest version of the Combattante is the Mk III which has been 'stretched' to provide space for a second 76mm. dual purpose cannon and four 21 in. wire-guided torpedo tubes aft, plus two twin 30mm. Emerlec-30 light AA mountings amidships. Four of these craft are operating with the Hellenic Navy.

9
CONSTITUCION CLASS

Federacion, one of six Constitucion class fast attack craft supplied to the Venezuelan Navy by Vosper Thornycroft in the mid-1970s. Three of these vessels, P12 Federacion, P14 Libertad and P16 Victoria are equipped with a 40mm. gun forward and two Otomat Mk.2 missile launches aft. The remaining three, P11 Constitucion, P13 Independencia and P15 Patria, carry a single Oto Melara 76/62 automatic cannon forward.

OTOMAT ANTI-SHIP MISSILE

Propelled by a Turbomeca gas-turbine, the Otomat missile has a range of 60 km. and a top speed of Mach 0.9. It is supplied in a special container which is also used as its launcher.

10
DABUR CLASS

This is an enlarged version of a boat built in the USA by the Swift Ship Co. of New Orleans to service oil rigs in the Caribbean. During the Vietnam war a military variant was built for the US Navy for coastal patrol in Vietnam then subsequently the Israeli Navy ordered a 65 ft model for anti-infiltration patrol along Israel's Mediterranean and Red Sea coasts. Normal armament comprises two 20mm. cannon, one forward, one aft, and two .50cal. machine-guns mounted on the open bridge.

11
NASTY

Series production of this 45 knot, Norwegian designed torpedo-boat is being undertaken in Turkey. Introduced in the early 1960s, Nasty class craft were built initially in Norway and the United States. A number have seen service with the US, West German, Greek and Norwegian Navies. Extensive use was made of this type during the Vietnam war. First craft of the Turkish series is the Girne, which is armed with four 21in. torpedo tubes and two 40mm. AA mounts. Nineteen craft of this design are in service in Norway, where it is known as the Tjelde class.

12
FLAGSTAFF II

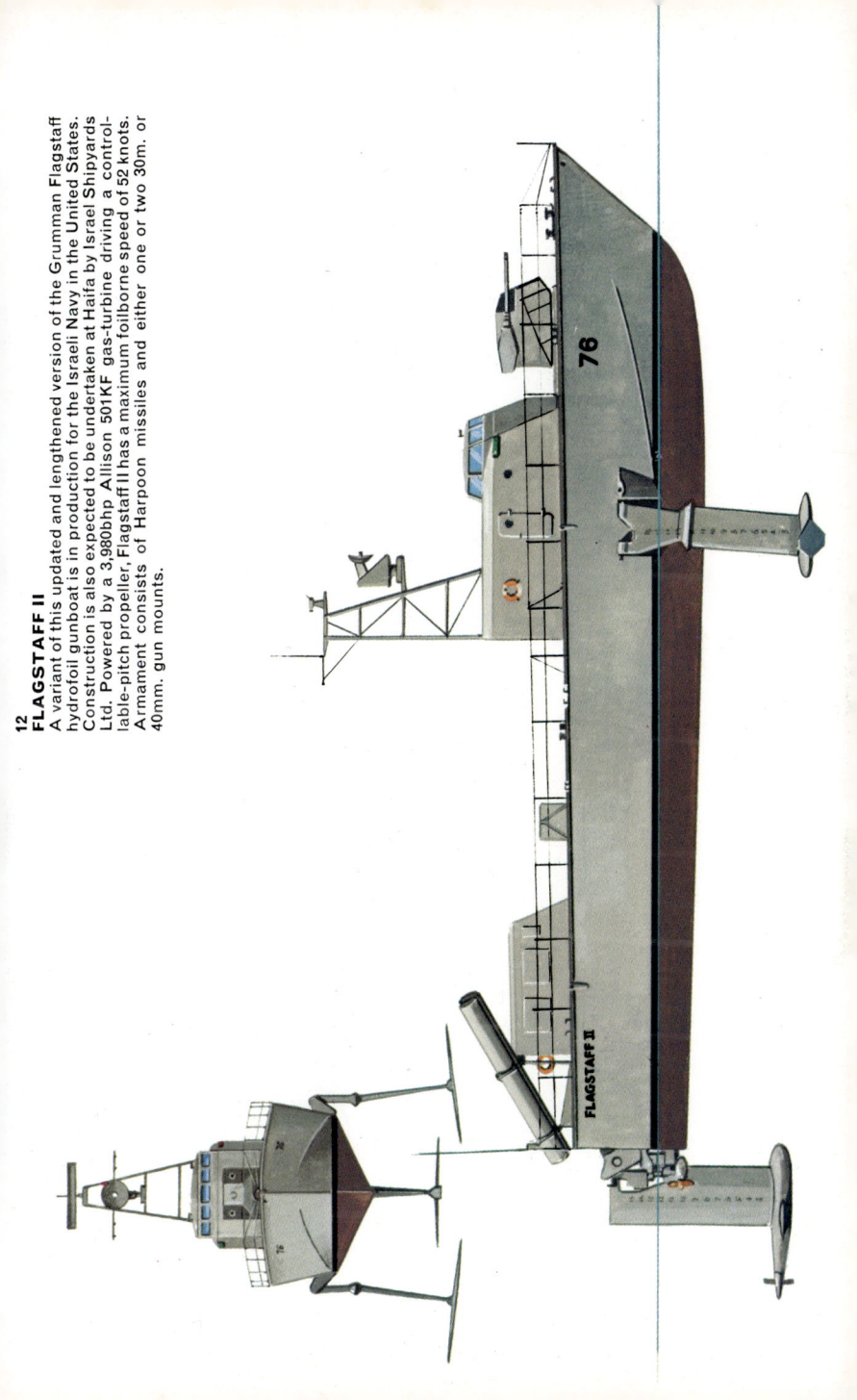

A variant of this updated and lengthened version of the Grumman Flagstaff hydrofoil gunboat is in production for the Israeli Navy in the United States. Construction is also expected to be undertaken at Haifa by Israel Shipyards Ltd. Powered by a 3,980bhp Allison 501KF gas-turbine driving a controllable-pitch propeller, Flagstaff II has a maximum foilborne speed of 52 knots. Armament consists of Harpoon missiles and either one or two 30mm. or 40mm. gun mounts.

13
FRECCIA CLASS
This multi-duty craft can be operated as a gunboat, fast minelayer, missile-craft or torpedo boat. Conversion from any one of these rôles to another to suit a change in tactical situation takes about 24 hours. A single 4250shp, Rolls-Royce Marine Proteus gas-turbine is fitted for sprint performance and two 3,800bhp diesels for cruising. Top speed is in excess of 40 knots. *Left*: Detail of one of the three 40mm. Breda/Bofors Type 107 naval mountings on the Freccia. The mounting consists of a single 40mm. L/70 rapid-fire cannon and a 32-round magazine. Firing can be controlled either remotely or manually.

14
GUACOLDA CLASS
Four of these Lürssen-designed fast attack torpedo craft were built for the Chilean Navy in Spain in the mid-1960s. Armament comprises four 21in. (533mm.) torpedoes and two 40mm. gun mounts. Main engines are two 2,400bhp MTU diesels. Top speed is about 32 knots.

15
HAUK CLASS

This new and highly formidable class of Norwegian missile craft carries six of the latest long-range Penguin missiles, four 21in. (533mm.) torpedoes, one 40mm. mount forward and a 20mm. gun aft. The class is similar in external appearance to the earlier Snögg class, but displays a variety of technical improvements, including the adoption of a new combat and weapons control system. Hauk cruises at 34 knots and has a range of 440 miles.

16
HU CHWAN CLASS

This highly successful hydrofoil torpedo-boat has been under construction at the Hutang Shipyard, Shanghai, since 1966, and in Romania since 1973. Apart from China, which has some 60-70 in service, Hu Chwan are operated by Albania (32), Pakistan (6), Romania (10), Tanzania (4) and Zaire (3). The Hu Chwan is basically a standard displacement torpedo-boat hull to which a main bow foil and pitch-stability sub foil have been added to aid the attainment of higher speeds in calm conditions. At high speed all but the stern is raised clear of the water, permitting speeds of up to 55 knots to be attained in favourable sea states.

17
HUGIN CLASS (ORIGINALLY JÄGAREN)
Hugin (P151) is one of a class of seventeen fast attack missile craft under construction in Norway for the Swedish Navy. Main armament is normally six Penguin Mk2 missiles, although these can be exchanged for mines or four 21in. (533mm.) torpedoes should the tactical situation demand it. A Philips PEAB 9LV200 Mk2 automated missile and weapon control system is installed enabling several aircraft or surface targets to be attacked simultaneously.

18
JAGUAR CLASS

Lürssen's first large post-war order for torpedo-boats was for Plejad class craft for the Swedish Navy in 1954. When it was re-established in 1955, the West German Navy contracted Lürssen to build a similar design which became known as the Type 140-141 Jaguar class. Thirty were completed. Ten were subsequently converted into Type 142 Zobel fast attack torpedo craft, and a number of others were transferred to overseas navies including Ecuador, Ghana and Turkey.

19
ISKU

Isku was built as a training vessel for the crews of nine Osa class missile craft ordered for the Finnish Navy. The Osas, built in the Soviet Union, are fitted with Finnish electronics. Isku was apparently employed initially as a test bed for the development of the Finnish designed weapons and fire control systems, then for training crews in its use. Isku is basically a mock-up of the deckhouse and missile launchers of a standard Osa II mounted on a flat-bottomed landing craft hull.

20
KARTAL CLASS

A total of sixteen Jaguar fast attack torpedo craft have been either built for the Turkish Navy by Lürssen as the Kartal class or transferred there by the West German Navy. Four of these, Albatros, Meltem, Pelikan and Simsek have been re-armed with Harpoon anti-ship missiles. Four 3,000bhp MTU diesels give the Kartal a maximum speed of 42 knots.

21
KRIS CLASS
Badek, one of fourteen Kris class FBBs, built by Vosper Thornycroft for the Malaysian Navy. Armed with 240mm. cannon, these craft are employed for coastal patrol, contraband control and fishery protection. Fitted with Vosper stabilizers, it is said to be the smallest patrol boat capable of maintaining a speed of 25 knots in normal conditions on the open sea.

KOMAR CLASS

First of the 'new generation' of missile-equipped fast patrol boats, the Komar was developed during the late 1950s to threaten US Navy carriers approaching Soviet occupied shorelines. The idea of pairing the Soviet Navy's first operational anti-ship missile, the 'Styx' with the wooden hull of a P6 class torpedo boat is generally credited to Soviet Admiral of the Fleet Sergey Gorshkov. By 1974 some twenty-five had been delivered to the Soviet Navy and another hundred and eighteen had been transferred to overseas navies, including those of Algeria, China, Egypt, Indonesia, North Korea, Syria and Vietnam. In addition eight Komars have been built in Egypt. Six of these are being re-armed by Vosper Thornycroft with Otomat missiles operated by a Marconi-Sperry fire control system.

23
Mo1

Latest displacement fast attack torpedo-boat to enter service with the Soviet Navy, Mo1 is generally thought to be a replacement for the Shershen class which was introduced in the early 1960s. Like Shershen, Mo1 is designed to operate on open seas. Vessels of this type have been transferred by the Soviet Navy to Somalia and Sri Lanka.

NANUSHKA

Biggest vessel described in these pages, Nanushka is classified by the Soviet Navy not as a patrol craft but as a 'missile cutter'. Its loaded displacement of 850 tons or more places it within the corvette category, but because of its strong similarity in outline and purpose to the Komar and Osa, the first two members of Admiral Gorshkov's 'giant killer' family, it was decided to include it as a fast attack missile craft. Series production of Nanushka is underway at a rate of about three a year. Although normally deployed around the Soviet coastline, units are occasionally seen in the North Sea and Mediterranean. Six SS-N-9 anti-ship missiles are carried. The normal range of this missile is thought to be 60n. miles, but this could be extended with mid-course guidance by aircraft or helicopter.

LANCE/SPEAR/SWORD/TRACKER

LANCE
Intended for general patrol duties by police and custom authorities, Lance is available as either a fast patrol boat or fast gun boat. In the latter rôle a 20mm. cannon is mounted on the aft deck.

SPEAR
Another design by Fairey Marine Ltd, Spear is widely employed by police and customs for fast patrol duties.

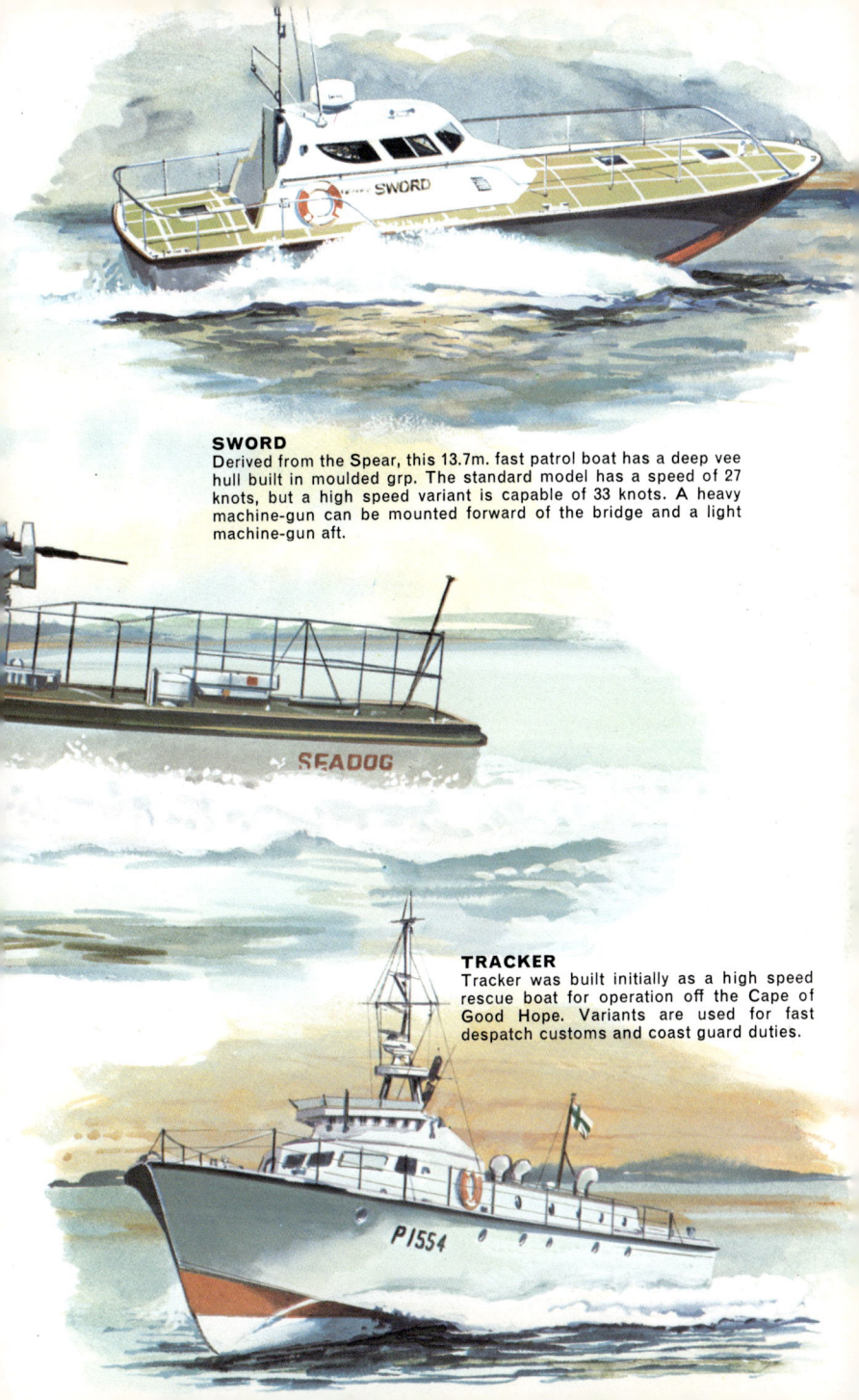

SWORD
Derived from the Spear, this 13.7m. fast patrol boat has a deep vee hull built in moulded grp. The standard model has a speed of 27 knots, but a high speed variant is capable of 33 knots. A heavy machine-gun can be mounted forward of the bridge and a light machine-gun aft.

TRACKER
Tracker was built initially as a high speed rescue boat for operation off the Cape of Good Hope. Variants are used for fast despatch customs and coast guard duties.

26
OSA CLASS

The world's most widely used missile craft, Osa was the second of the Soviet Navy's missile firing patrol boats to enter service and the first with a steel hull. Four large hooded Styx missile launchers are arranged in two pairs abreast of the deckhouse. Two variants of the Osa are in service, the Mk 1 with slab sided launchers for SS-N-2A or 2B missiles and the more recent Osa II with elongated dustbin shaped launchers. About 120 Osas are in service with the Soviet Navy, and at least another 155 have been transferred to other navies.

27
P.6 CLASS
Nearly 300 fast attack torpedo-boats of this class were built by the Soviet Unoin before production ended in 1960. Of wooden construction, the P.6 is powered by four 1,200bhp M.50, M.400 or similar marinised diesels which provide a top speed of 43 knots. A later variant the P.8 was redesigned for anti-submarine warfare. It was equipped with a bow hydrofoil only and fitted with a gas-turbine engine for improved 'sprint' performance. The craft illustrated was produced for Egypt.

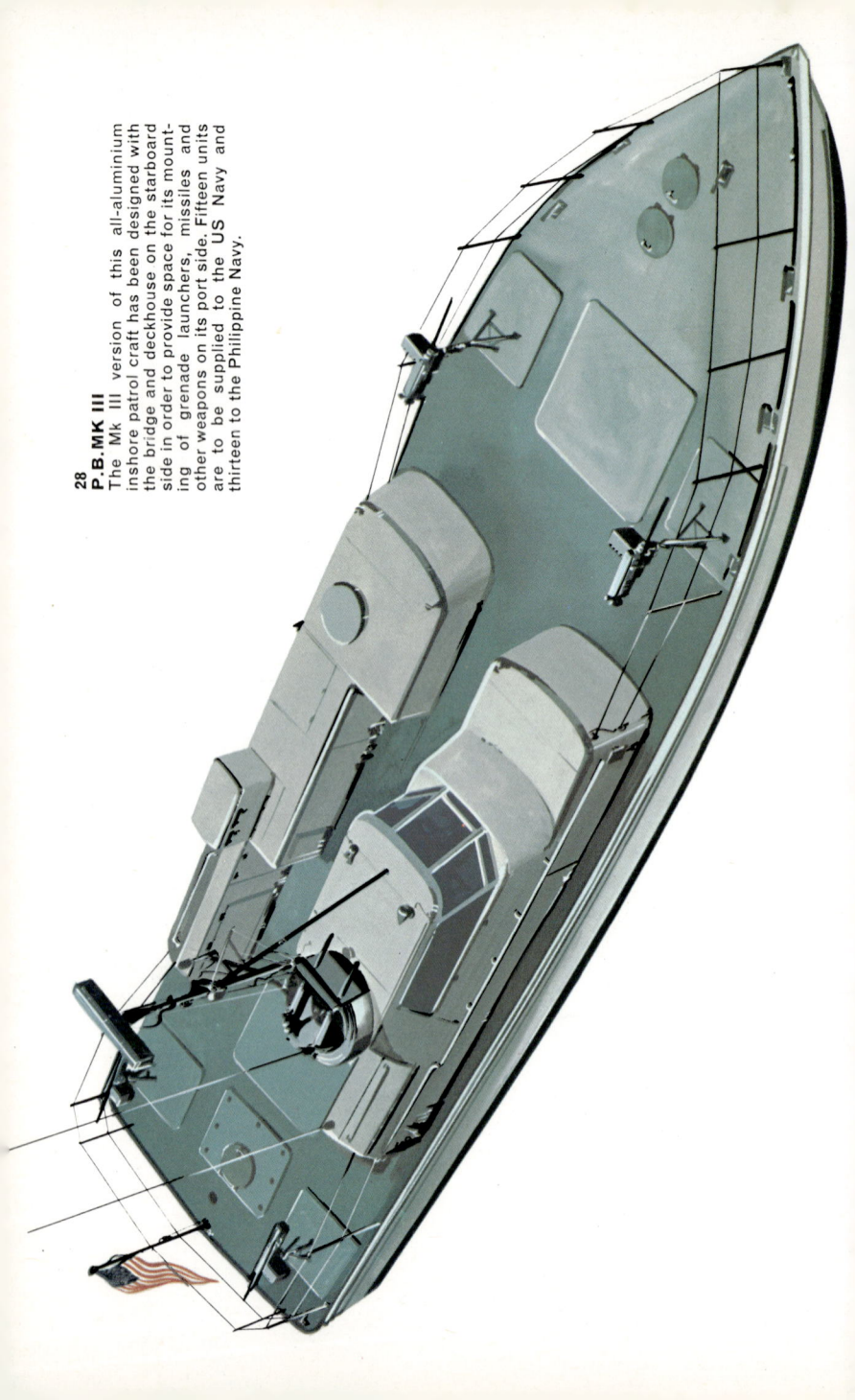

28
P.B. MK III
The Mk III version of this all-aluminium inshore patrol craft has been designed with the bridge and deckhouse on the starboard side in order to provide space for its mounting of grenade launchers, missiles and other weapons on its port side. Fifteen units are to be supplied to the US Navy and thirteen to the Philippine Navy.

29
PAEK KU CLASS
One of the most sophisticated fast strike craft in service today is the US Navy's Asheville class, of which the Paek Ku is a derivative. Designated Patrol Ship, Multi-mission (PSMM), the Asheville, in various forms, has been adopted by the navies of South Korea, Taiwan, Saudi Arabia and Indonesia. Power for the eight-strong Paek Ku class is provided by six TF35 gas-turbines driving two shafts, each with a cp propeller. The gas-turbines can be introduced singly, in pairs or collectively, offering a wide range of power settings.

30
PCHELA CLASS
Employed by the KGB frontier police in the Baltic, Black Sea and Caspian Sea, the Pchela hydrofoil fast patrol boat is armed with two remotely operated twin machine-gun mounts and depth charges. Derived from the Strela hydrofoil passenger ferry, it is powered by two 12-cylinder vee-type diesels and cruises at about 32 knots.

31
PERKASA CLASS

Built by Vosper Ltd for the Malaysian Navy in the mid-1960s, the four Perkasa class triple-screw fast attack craft were armed originally with four 21in. torpedoes. In 1971 they were re-armed with eight Aérospatiale SS-12M close-range, surface-to-surface wire-guided missiles. Maximum speed of the Perkasa, which is powered by three Rolls-Royce Marine Proteus gas-turbines, is in excess of 40 knots. *Left:* The SS-12M wire-guided missile. Maximum range is 6000m. Impact speed, 182 knots.

32
PHM CLASS

The USS Pegasus, first of the Boeing/NATO PHM (Patrol Hydrofoil Missile) class vessels was commissioned into service with the US Navy in July 1977, becoming the first hydrofoil to be designated a United States Ship. Five follow-on craft will be delivered between January 1981 and February 1982. Four of the follow-on craft will be assigned to a PHM squadron operating with the US Sixth Fleet in the Mediterranean and specialising in anti-submarine warfare in coastal waters.

33
PLEJAD CLASS

When designing this outstandingly successful class of 45m. torpedo-boats for the Royal Swedish Navy in the early 1950s Lürssen was able to draw on its substantial experience with the range of Schnellboots (E-boats) it had built for the German Navy during World War II. A slightly larger and more powerful variant was ordered by the West German Navy for its own use in 1955. Powered by three 3,000bhp MTU diesels and with a fully-loaded displacement of 170 tons, the Plejad has a maximum speed of 37.5 knots.

34
RADE KONCAR

The first fast attack missile craft to be built in Yugoslavia, Rade Koncar is the first of a class of ten. Equipment from both Europe and the Soviet Union is employed in its outfitting. The main engines are two Marine Proteus gas-turbines from the UK; its cruising engines are supplied by MTU in West Germany; its guns and electronics come from Sweden, and its SS-N-2B missiles are supplied by the Soviet Union.

35
RESHEF CLASS

Built by the state-owned Israel Shipyards Ltd, Haifa, Reshef combines the range of a destroyer with a maximum continuous cruising speed of 25-30 knots. It is designed to protect Israel's narrow shipping lanes extending from the home coastline to the Eastern shores of Sicily, and from Sharm-el-Sheik, at the mouth of the Gulf of Aqaba, to the mouth of the Red Sea in the Straits of Bab-al-Handab. Main armament generally comprises two 76mm. Oto Melara dual-purpose cannon, six Gabriel and four Harpoon missiles. *Left:* Gabriel missile.

36
SAAR CLASS

Twelve of these fast attack missile craft were built for the Israeli Navy by Constructions Mécaniques de Normandie, at Cherbourg, between 1966-69. Designed by Lürssen as torpedo-boats, they were re-armed with Israel's own sea-skimming missile, the Gabriel, on arrival in Haifa. Various weapons refits have resulted in the following configurations: Saar I, 240mm. AA guns and five Gabriels; Saar II, 140mm. AA mount and eight Gabriels; Saar III, one Oto Melara 76mm. dual-purpose cannon and six Gabriels. Four torpedo tubes can be fitted if required.

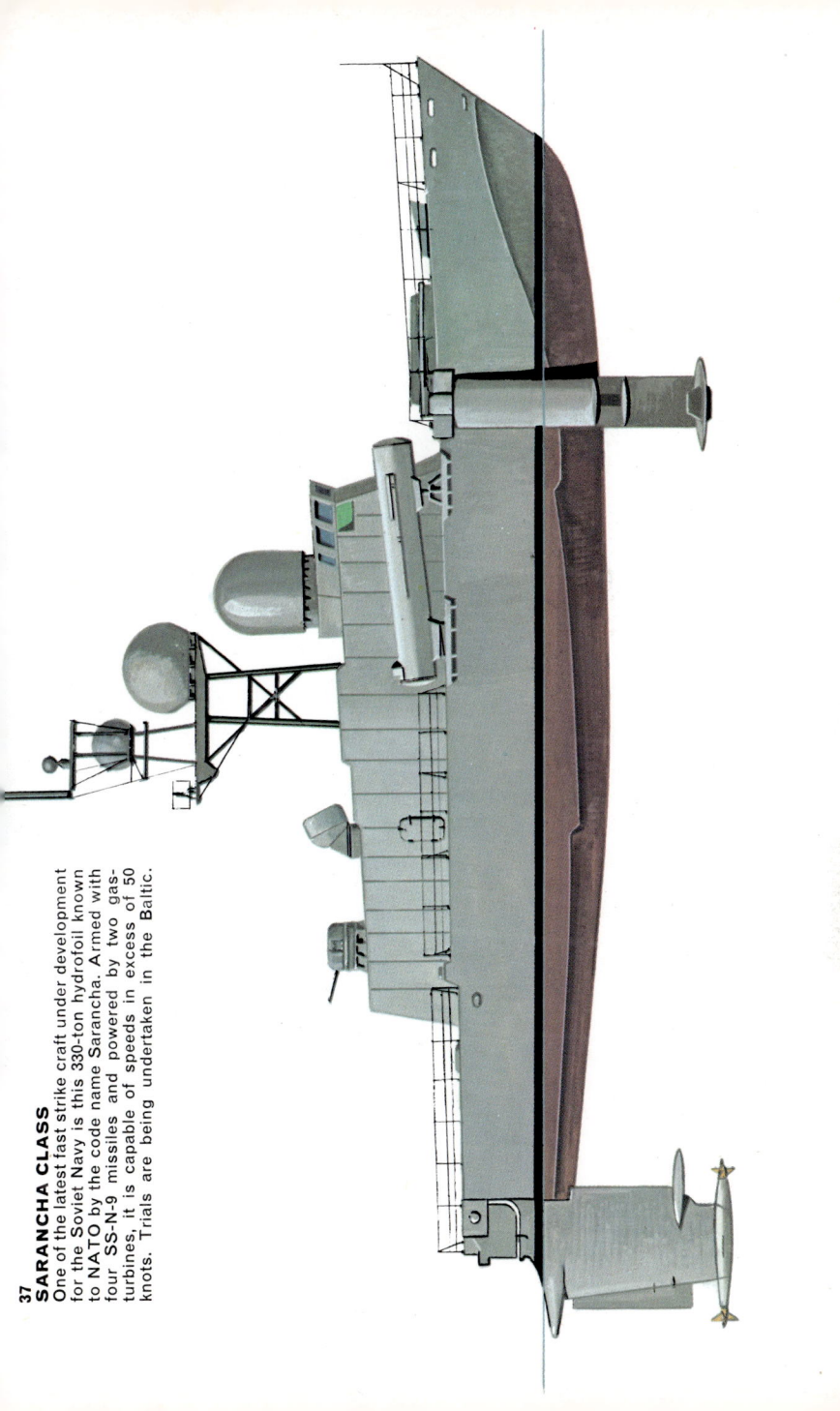

37
SARANCHA CLASS
One of the latest fast strike craft under development for the Soviet Navy is this 330-ton hydrofoil known to NATO by the code name Sarancha. Armed with four SS-N-9 missiles and powered by two gas-turbines, it is capable of speeds in excess of 50 knots. Trials are being undertaken in the Baltic.

38 SCIMITAR CLASS

The twin-screw, gas-turbine powered Scimitar and its two sister craft, Cutlass and Sabre, are employed by the Royal Navy to simulate attacks on NATO naval forces by hostile missile craft. Although these craft normally operate unarmed a forward gun can be fitted should it be required for operational purposes. Provision is also made for the installation of a third Proteus engine, as on the earlier Brave class from which the Scimitar was developed.

39 SEA WOLF CLASS

Sea Wolf and Sea Lion, the first two units of this Gabriel-armed fast strike class were built for the Republic of Singapore Navy by Lürssen Werft at Vegesack. The remaining four, Sea Dragon (pictured below), Sea Tiger, Sea Hawk and Sea Scorpion, were built locally during 1972-75 by the Singapore Shipbuilding and Engineering Co. one of Lürssen's overseas licencees. In addition to their five Gabriel missiles, each craft mounts one 57mm. Bofors gun forward and one 40mm. gun aft.

40
SHANGHAI CLASS

Production of this 39m. multi-purpose fast gunboat has been underway at the Shanghai Naval Yard and other Chinese yards since the early 1960s. More than 350 had been completed by mid 1977, more than 60 of which had been transferred to the navies of emerging countries in Africa, Asia and the Far East. A number of variants are in service, in each differing in bridge outline, armament and the position of the gun mounts. Mine rails, torpedo tubes and depth charges can be carried.

41
SHERSHEN CLASS
Fifty or more of these fast attack torpedo-boats are in service with the Soviet Navy. Its armament comprises four 21in. torpedoes, two twin 30mm. L/65 automatic cannon mounts and twelve depth charges.

Left: The Penguin anti-ship guided missile. Inertial guidance is employed for the cruising phase and passive infra-red homing guides it to the target in the terminal phase. Cruising speed is Mach 0.7 and its range is 11n. miles.

42
SNÖGG CLASS

Employing a similar hull to that of the earlier Storm class missile-boats, the Snögg class differs mainly in its weapons fit. Instead of the six Penguin anti-ship missiles carried by the Storm, it carries four Penguins and four 21in. torpedoes. Six vessels of this class were built by Båtservice, Mandel, Norway, for the Norwegian Navy between 1970-71.

43
SOLOVEN CLASS
Powered by three Proteus gas-turbines, the Danish Navy's Søløven class is similar in design and construction to Libya's Susa and Malaya's Perkasa. The first two units in the Søløven class were built by Vosper Ltd and the remaining three by the Royal Dockyard, Copenhagen. Maximum speed is in excess of 54 knots.

SPARVIERO CLASS

First fully operational hydrofoil missilecraft was the little Sparviero which was delivered to the Italian Navy in July 1974. An order was placed by the Italian Navy for a further six in February 1976. Derived from the Boeing Tucumcari, the Sparviero is powered by a gas-turbine driven waterjet and has a top speed of 50 knots. Armament comprises a 76 mm. Oto Melara automatic cannon on the foredeck and two Otomat Sea Killer or Exocet missiles aft. To simplify maintenance and assist hullborne manoeuvring in shallow waters, all three foils are retractable.

45
SPICA T121 CLASS

This stern view of a Spica T121 shows three of the six 21in. torpedo tubes and the single Bofors h/70 57mm. multi-purpose gun forward. Two twin missile launchers are to be installed in place of the aft pair of torpedo tubes. Note the air intake hood for the three Proteus gas-turbines, aft of the bridge superstructure, and the three transom exhausts. Transom gas-turbine exhausts can result in increased speed, an extra knot at 50 knots on a three Proteus engined fast patrol boat is reckoned to be typical of the advantage gained.

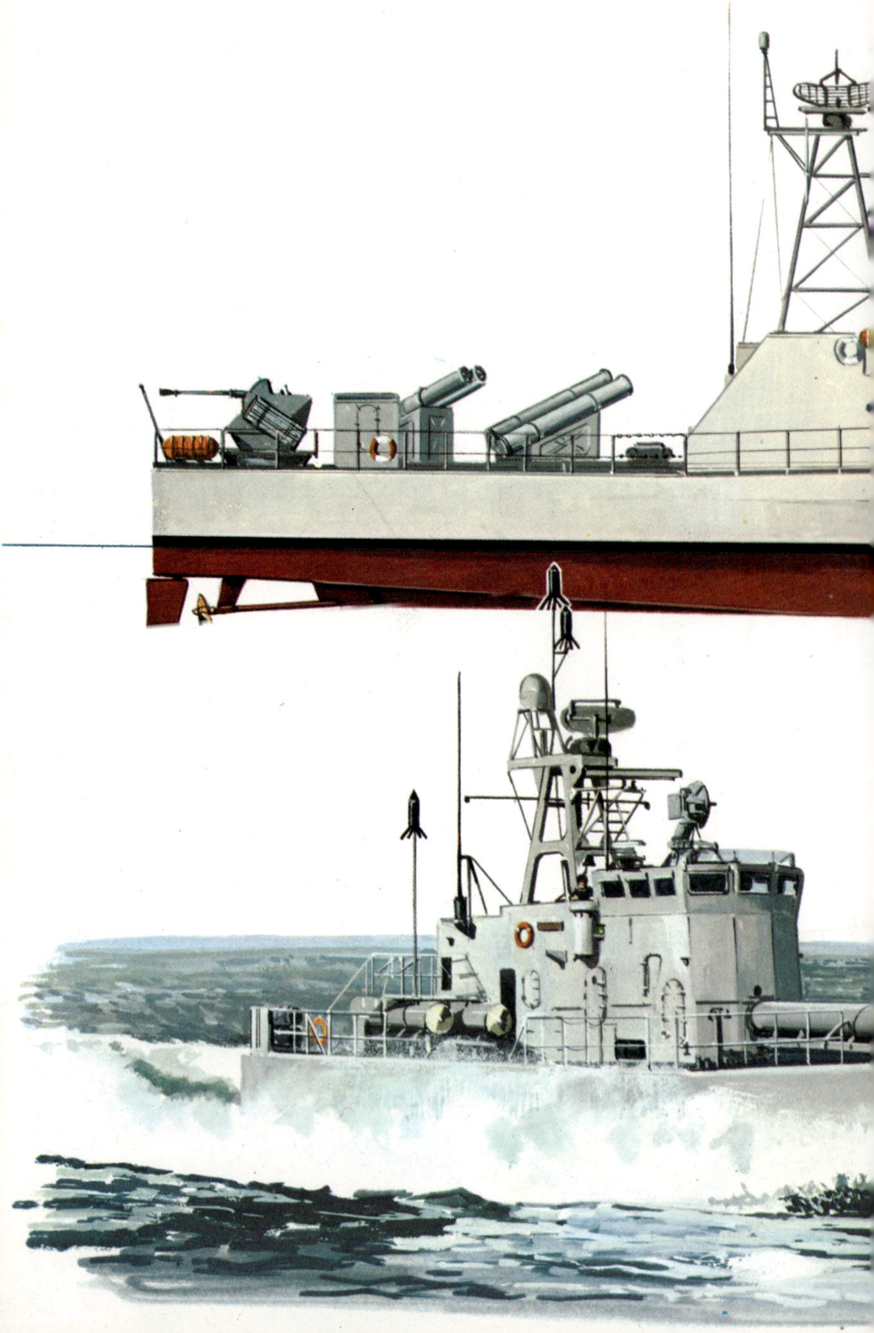

46
SPICA-M CLASS
Based on the hull of the Spica II, the Spica-M is intended for export and has been specially adapted for the world's smaller navies. Major design changes include substituting diesel engines for the three gas-turbines and installing four Exocet missiles in the place of the torpedoes carried by Spica II. The first four Spica-Ms have been ordered by Malaysia.

47
SPICA II CLASS. *Below.*
T131 Norrköping, one of twelve Spica II torpedo-boats on order for the Royal Swedish Navy. This highly successful craft is powered by three Marine Proteus gas-turbines, each driving a controllable-pitch propeller. It can be operated on one, two or three engines according to the speed required.

48
STENKA CLASS

Based on the steel hull of the Osa, Stenka is employed by the Soviet Union on offshore, anti-submarine patrols. Main armament comprises four 405mm. ASW torpedoes and depth charges. Two 30mm. automatic AA mounts are fitted, one forward, one aft. Maximum speed is 33 knots.

49
STORM CLASS
Primary armament of Norway's Storm class is the Penguin missile, which is designed to inflict as much damage as possible on vessels up to the size of a destroyer. Twenty units were built by Bergens MV and Westermoen A/S between 1966-68.

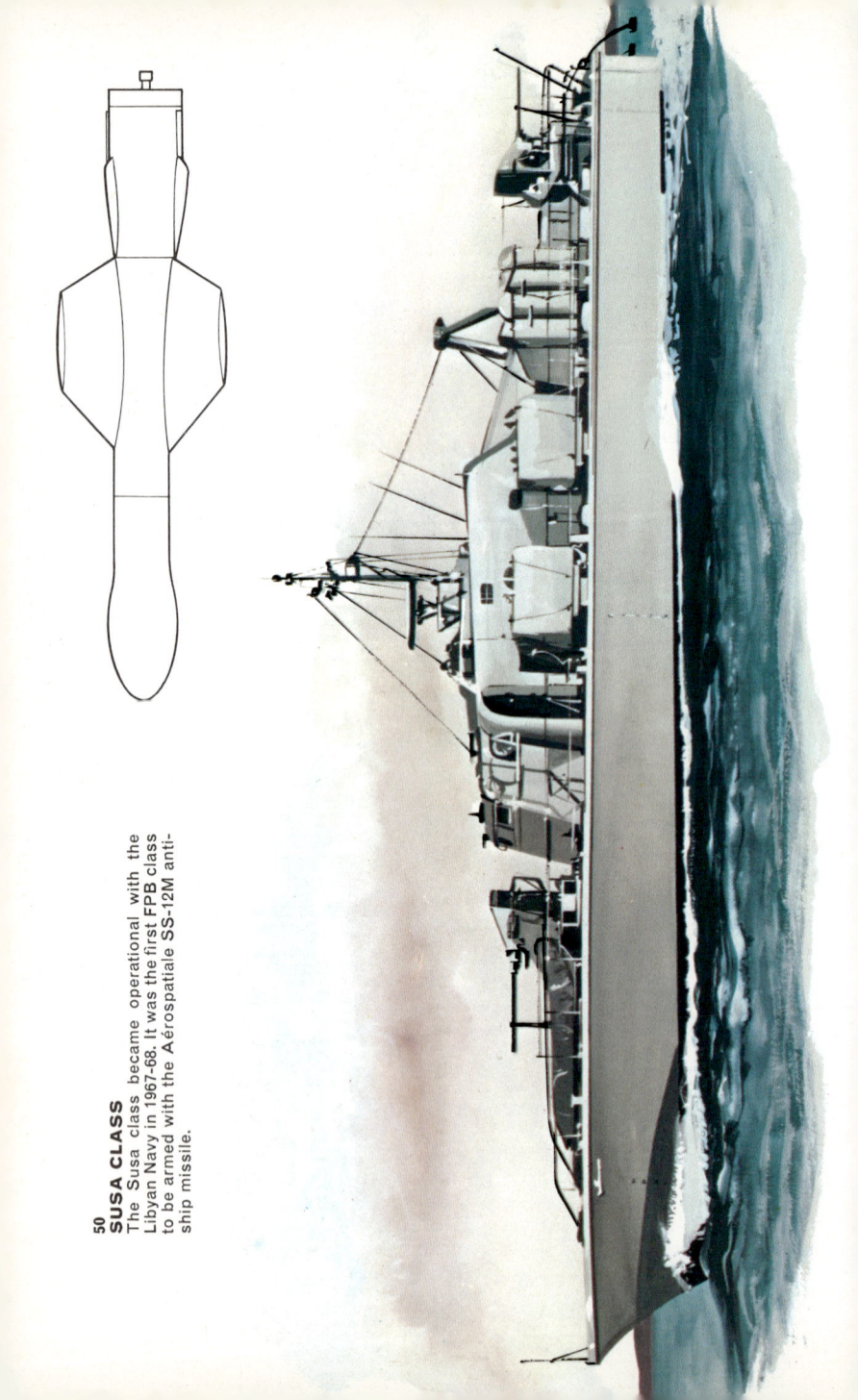

50
SUSA CLASS
The Susa class became operational with the Libyan Navy in 1967-68. It was the first **FPB** class to be armed with the Aérospatiale **SS-12M** anti-ship missile.

51
TENACITY CLASS
Employed by the Royal Navy for fishery protection and counter missilecraft exercises, Tenacity began its life as a test and demonstration craft. Designed to attack much larger craft, its main weapon was intended to be the Contraves Sea Killer missile, with a range of 20km. and the hitting power of a 6in. shell. One of the features of the craft is its endurance. It is capable of remaining at sea for up to a week in any reasonable weather.

52
TJELD

Nineteen Tjeld class torpedo-boats have been in service with the Norwegian Navy since the early 1960s. Known originally as the 'Nasty' class, they were designed and built by Batservis of Mandel, Norway, and are powered by British-built 18-cylinder Napier Deltic turbocharged diesels. The Tjeld mounts one 40mm. gun forward, one 20mm. gun aft and four 21in. torpedoes. Maximum speed is 45 knots.

TURYA CLASS

Based on the welded steel hull of the Osa, this 230-ton hydrofoil torpedo-boat is entering service at the rate of four to five units per year. More than twenty-five have been built. As with the P.8 and Hu Chwan, a surface-piercing trapeze foil is attached to the bow only. At between 20 and 23 knots, depending on loading and sea conditions, the foil generates sufficient lift to raise a substantial part of the lower hull clear of the water, thus reducing hydrodynamic drag and providing a sprint speed of 40-45 knots.

54
TYPE 143

Mixed wooden and light alloy construction is employed in this new class of fast strike craft designed and built for use by the West German Navy on the Baltic. A fully integrated command and fire control system is fitted to permit direct automatic information exchange with other surface vessels, aircraft and land bases and enable the flotilla commander to obtain target instructions. Four launchers are provided for Exocet missiles and two 21in. torpedo tubes are located aft

55
TYPE 148

Types 143 and 148 were built to replace the West German Navy's earlier Jaguar torpedo-boats which would have been incapable of countering attacks on the approaches to the Baltic by missile craft. The Type 148 is based on the French-built Combattante II, with a 2m. extension to provide room for four Exocets amidships.

Right: The Exocet MM38 sea-skimming missile with radar homing head. Speed is Mach 0.93 and range is 42km.

56
WILLEMOES CLASS

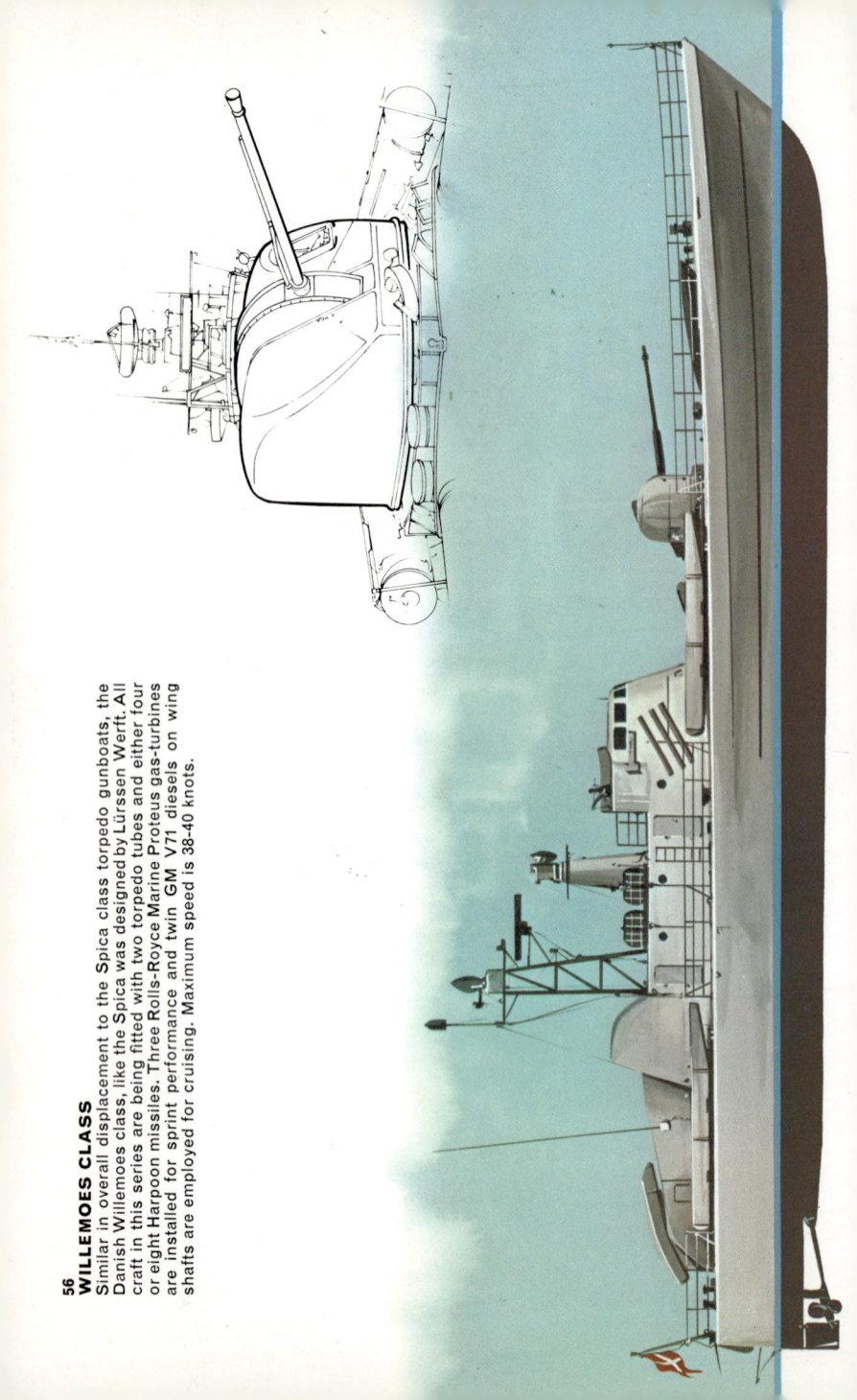

Similar in overall displacement to the Spica class torpedo gunboats, the Danish Willemoes class, like the Spica was designed by Lürssen Werft. All craft in this series are being fitted with two torpedo tubes and either four or eight Harpoon missiles. Three Rolls-Royce Marine Proteus gas-turbines are installed for sprint performance and twin GM V71 diesels on wing shafts are employed for cruising. Maximum speed is 38-40 knots.

57 WISLA CLASS

Fifteen of these Polish-built torpedo-boats are in service. Main armament comprises four 21in. (533 mm.) torpedoes. A fully-automatic twin 30mm. mounting of Soviet design is provided for AA defence.

Left: The L/65 twin 30mm. automatic AA mounting employed with Drum Tilt fire control radar and used widely on Soviet missile craft and other smaller boats. Range is about 3-4,000m. and rate of fire 500 rounds/minute/barrel.

P 52

58
VOSPER 52M FAST MISSILE BOAT
This new design from Vosper Thornycroft has four Otomat missile launchers, an Oto Melara 76/62 mount forward and a Breda 40 h70 twin mounting aft. Construction is in welded mild steel with weatherdeck and superstructure in seawater resistant aluminium alloy. The propulsion machinery comprises a diesel-driven quadruple screw arrangement, each shaft being driven by a 4,000hp Paxman Valenta diesel through a reverse reduction gearbox. Maximum speed is 40 knots.

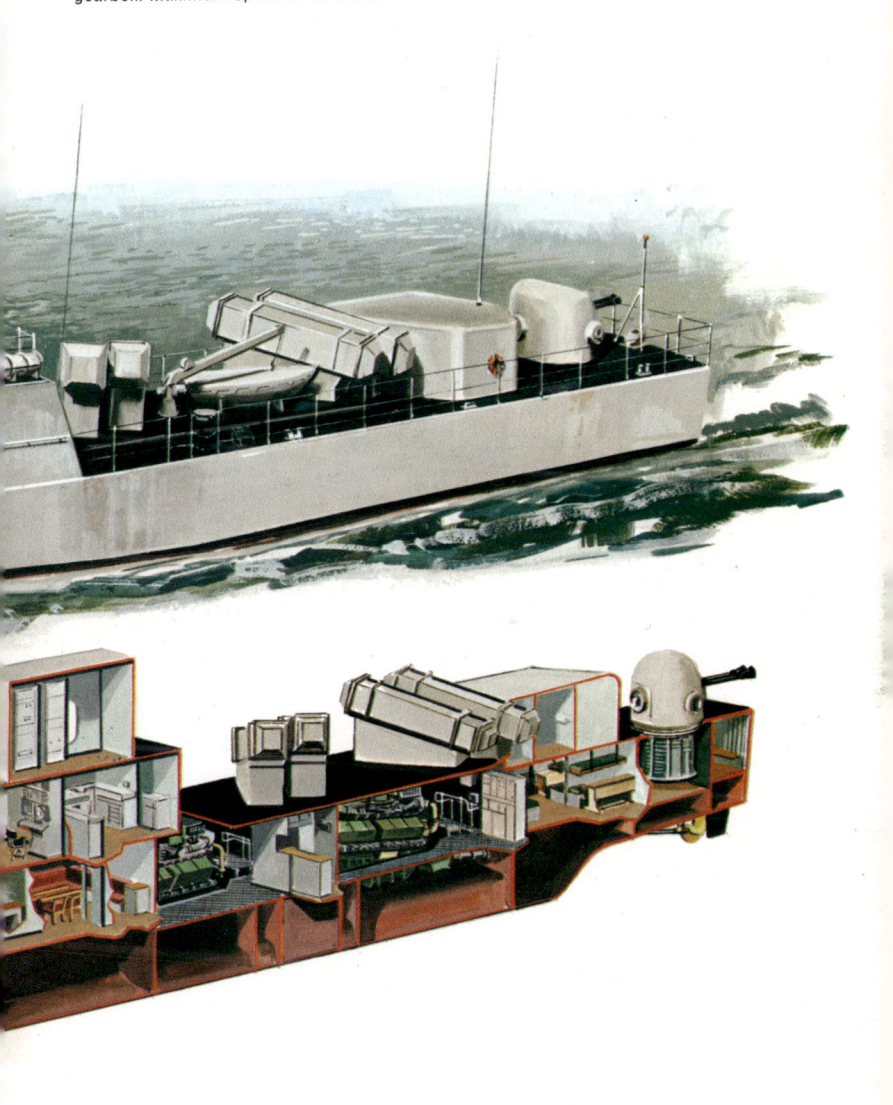

ZOBEL CLASS
The Type 142 Zobel class torpedo-boats are converted Type 140-141 Jaguar class vessels which have been re-armed with Seal wire-guided torpedoes. The torpedoes are guided to their targets by computer or manual control or by a self-homing system installed in the torpedo itself.

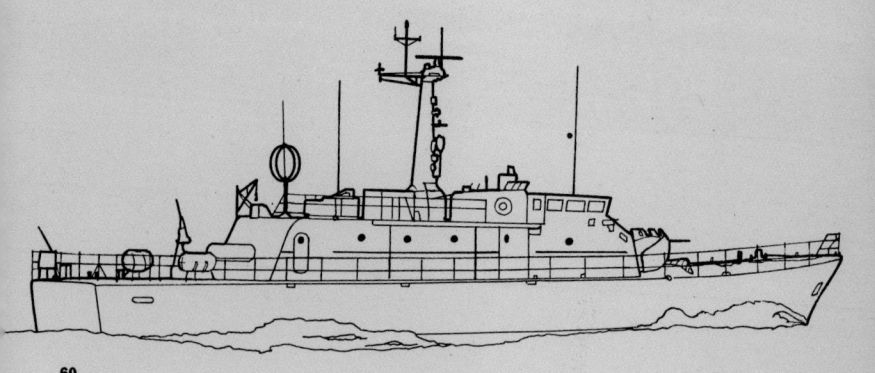

**60
TRIDENT**
Armed with six SS 12 wire-guided missiles and one 40mm. cannon, the Trident is one of a class of four 130-ton Fast Patrol Boats in service with the French Navy.

**61
HAI DAU.** *Below.*
This new addition to the sea defences of the Peoples Republic of China is armed with six SS-M-2 missiles and two twin 57mm. automatic cannon.

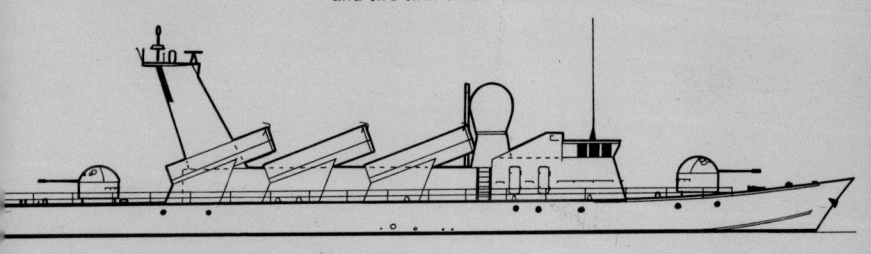

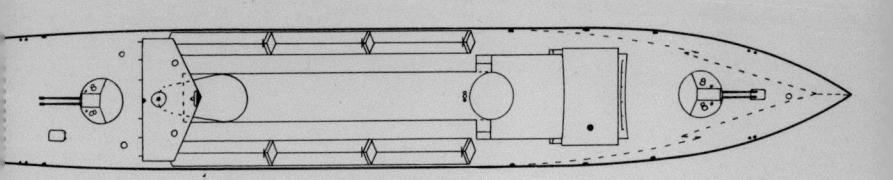

Basic WS80 System

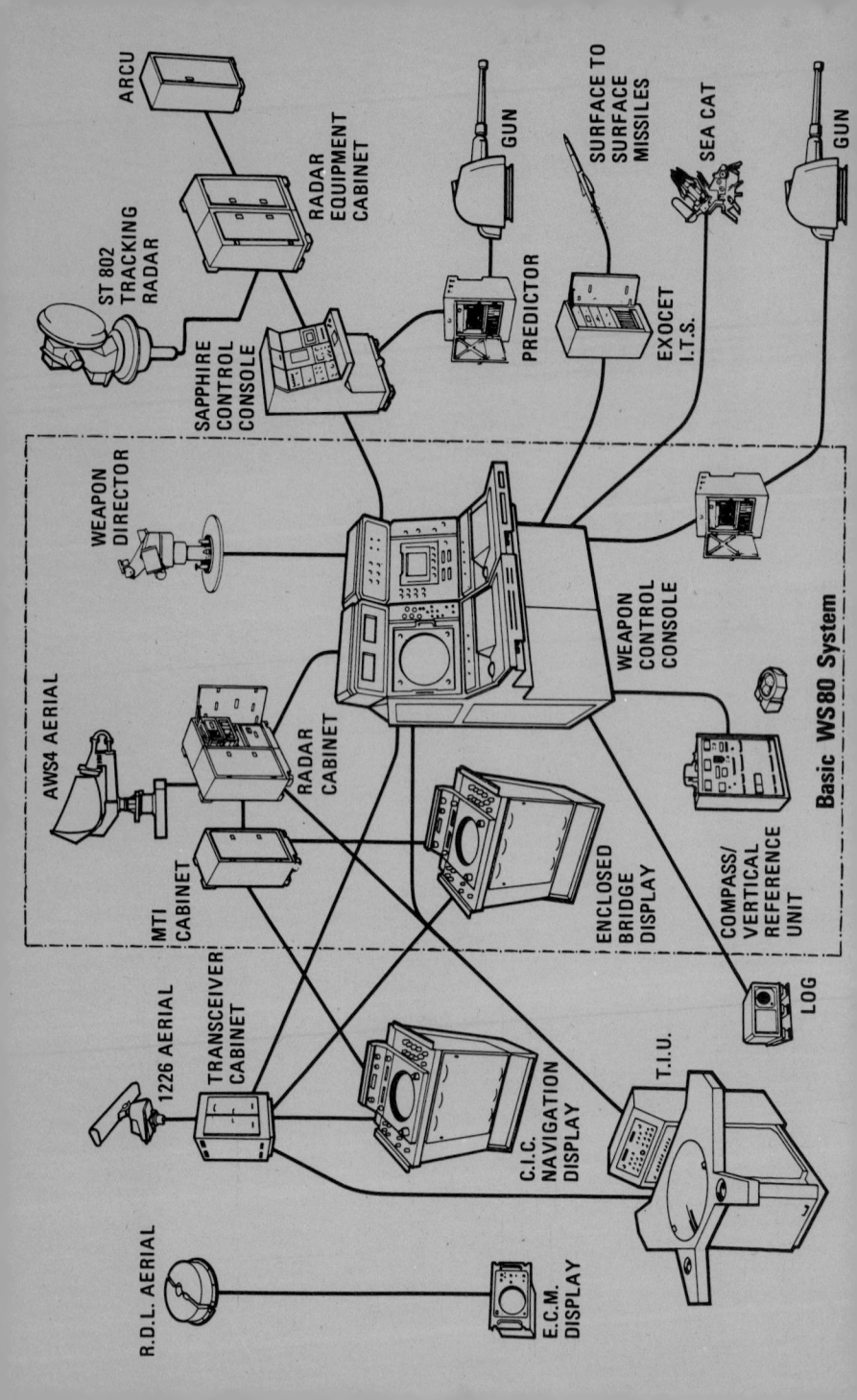

1 **Asheville**, U.S.A.
The Asheville class of patrol gunboats (PG) was built to an operational requirement which grew out of the need by the U.S. Navy for high performance gunboats at the time of the Cuban missile crisis in the early 1960s. They were designed to undertake patrol, blockade, support and surveillance duties and by 1971 seventeen vessels of this class were in service, although most have since been either 'retired' or transferred to overseas navies.

The Asheville was the biggest patrol boat class built for the U.S. Navy since the end of World War II and it was also the U.S. Navy's first warship to be powered by gas-turbines. Its powerplant was one of the first of the now popular combined diesel and gas-turbine (CODAG) systems, employing a 13,300 shp General Electric LM 2500 marinized gas-turbine for 'sprint' performance and twin 1,450 shp Cummins diesels for cruising. The source of power can be changed readily while underway and both the diesels and the gas-turbine can operate on either JP-5 or diesel fuel. Two other features of this class are their excellent manoeuvrability resulting from the use of controllable-pitch propellers and their astonishing power of acceleration when using the LM 2500 gas-turbine. A speed of 40 knots can be attained within one minute from full stop in the lower sea states.

Construction of this series was undertaken by Tacoma Boatbuilding Co. of Tacoma, Washington and Peterson Builders of Sturgeon Bay, Wisconsin. In 1971, the Benicia (PG96) was employed in the development of the Standard interim anti-ship missile (pending the introduction of the Harpoon). Subsequently Standard missiles were installed aboard the Antelope, Ready, Grand Rapids and Douglas. Currently the four craft are the only ones in active service with the U.S. Navy. Two more, however, PG92 Tacoma and PG93 Welch are being employed by the U.S. Navy as training vessels, in addition to which two have been transferred to Greece, two to Turkey and one to South Korea.

U.S. Navy
Pennant Nos/Class Names/Date of Commissioning
PG86 Antelope (4.11.67): PG87 Ready (6.1.68): PG98 Grand Rapids (5.9.70): PG100 Douglas (6.2.71).

Transfers
GREEK NAVY
Names awaited: former USS Beacon (PG99) and former USS Green Bay (PG101).

TURKISH NAVY
Bora formerly USS Surprise PG97, transferred 28.2.73.
Yildirim formerly USS Defiance PG95, transferred 11.6.73.

SOUTH KOREAN NAVY
Paek Ku (Seagull) II formerly USS Benicia PG96 transferred 15.10.71. First of the Paek Ku class. Subsequent craft, based on Asheville basic hull have six Avco Lycoming TF-35 gas turbines. (See separate entry.)

Powerplant: Codag system employing twin 1,450 hp Cummins diesels for cruising and a single 13,300 hp General Electric LM2500 marinized gas-turbine for 'sprint' performance. Controllable-pitch propellers. Four shafts.
Hull: Aluminium. Superstructure in aluminium and glass fibre.
Crew: Three officers and either 21 or 24 enlisted men.
Armament: Single 76 mm. gun mount forward and single 40 mm. gun aft plus four .50 machine-guns in two twin mounts on superstructure. The four vessels remaining in active service, Antelope, Ready, Grand Rapids and Douglas, are each equipped with two Standard interim ship-to-ship missile launchers which replace the aft 40 mm. cannon. Reloads are provided for each launcher.
Fire Control/Radar: Mk 87, the U.S. Navy's American-built

model of the Netherlands-designed HSA M22 fire control system is fitted to the Antelope and Ready. The other vessels are fitted with the Mk 63 Mod 29 gunfire control system and SPG-50 fire control radar.
Dimensions: Length overall 50.1 m. (164.5 ft): beam, 7.3 m. (23.8 ft): draft, 2.9 m. (9.5 ft).
Displacement: Standard 225 tons, fully loaded 235 tons.
Performance: Max. speed on diesel engines 16 knots: max. speed in excess of 40 knots. Range with diesel engines only 1,700 n. miles at 16 knots; with LM1500 gas-turbines, 325 n. miles at 37 knots.

2 **Al Fulk**, Oman.
This 37.5 m. Brooke Marine patrol craft is a development of the Seal, a steel-hulled, twin-screw long-range recovery and support craft designed and built by the company for the marine branch of the British Royal Air Force.

Al Fulk is one of a class of seven, commissioned between 1973 and 1977 by the Sultanate of Oman. Each unit is armed with an Oto Melara 76 mm. dual-purpose gun forward, an Oerlikon 20 mm. gun aft and two .5 machine-guns in the bridge wings. In November 1977, the first three in the class were rearmed with a twin MM38 Exocet launcher aft.

Pennant Nos/Class Names/Year of Commissioning
 B1 Al Bushra (1973): B2 Al Mansur (1973): B3 Al Nejah (1973): B4 Al Wafi (1977): B5 Al Fulk (1977): B6 Al Aul (1977): B7 Al Jabbar (1977).
Power Plant: Two 2,400 bhp Paxman Ventura diesels, each driving its own propeller shaft via a reverse/reduction gearbox.
Hull: All welded mild steel construction with aluminium alloy superstructure. Round bilge form with knuckle forward.

Crew: Arrangement for total complement of 27, depending on role. All living and working spaces air-conditioned.
Dimensions: Length overall 37.5 m. (123 ft): beam, 6.9 m. (22.5 ft): draught 1.7 m. (5.5 ft).
Displacement: Standard, 135 tons; fully loaded 153 tons.
Performance: Max. speed, 29 knots. Range 3,300 n. miles at 15 knots.

3 **Astrapi**, Greece.
A derivative of the Royal Navy's 52-knot Brave Borderer torpedo boat class of 1960, Astrapi employs a similar form of glued laminated wood construction and like the related Danish Søløven class is powered by three Rolls-Royce Proteus gas-turbines.

Originally built by Vosper for the navy of the German Federal Republic as the Strahl, Astrapi was transferred to the Royal Hellenic Navy in April 1967.

Pennant No./Class Name/Launch Date
   P20 Astrapi (10.1.62).
Power Plant: Three Rolls-Royce Proteus Marine gas-turbines, each rated at 3,620 bhp maximum and 2,960 continuous, on three separate shafts. Total fuel capacity, 25 tons.
Hull: Main hull and deck structure in glued laminated wood. Superstructure built in aluminium alloy.
Crew: CO, two officers, three POs and 16 ratings. Fully air-conditioned work and rest areas.
Armament: Torpedoes: 4 × 21 in. in side launchers. Guns: Two 40 mm.
Dimensions: Length overall 30.38 m. (99 ft 8 in.): beam 7.78 m. (25 ft 9 in.): draft aft 2.28 m. (7.3 ft).
Displacement: Standard 95 tons, fully loaded 110 tons.
Performance: Maximum speed 55.5 knots. Range (gas-turbines only fitted), 644 km. (400 miles). Long range deck tanks add further 160.93 km. (100 miles) to range.

4 **Azteca**, Mexico.

Azteca was designed in response to a Mexican Navy requirement for a fast patrol boat capable of performing fishing protection, coastguard and customs duties, rather than for a naval defence role. Its primary duty is to dissuade foreign fishing vessels from entering Mexican territorial waters. The specification called for a 34 m. craft capable of continuous operation in rough water off Mexico's Atlantic and Pacific seaboards, a speed of 24 knots and a shallow draught to permit its use in shallow waters. It was also essential that the structural design should be as straightforward as possible to ensure that it could be built at the developing Mexican shipyards. Sophisticated weaponry and electronics were rejected in favour of low initial cost, permitting more units to be built and operated within the available budget.

The consultancy/management contract was placed with the Marine Division of Associated British Machine Tool Makers Ltd (ABMTM) of London, which commissioned Cdr Peter Thornycroft FRINA to undertake the initial design. Following design discussions, the first stage of the contract was the construction of twenty-one vessels in Scottish shipyards, eleven by Ailsa Shipbuilding Co. of Troon, five at the Port Glasgow yard of James Lamont & Co., and the remaining five at Scott & Sons, Bowling. In June 1975 an order was placed for the construction of ten more of this class, seven at the Vera Cruz yard and three at Salina Cruz, Mexico. In 1976 the copyright of the design became the property of the Mexican government which plans to build a further fifty and to eventually offer the craft on the export market.

Pennant Nos/Name/Builder/Commissioning Date

PO1 Andres Quintana Roos (Ailsa) 1.11.74: PO2 Matias De Cordova (Scott) 22.10.74: PO3 Miguel Ramos Arizpe (Ailsa) 23.12.74: PO4 Jose Maria Izazgu (Ailsa) 19.12.74:

PO5 Juan Bautista Morales (Scott) 19.12.74: PO6 Ignacio Lopez Rayon (Ailsa) 19.12.74: PO7 Manuel Crecencio Rejon (Ailsa) 4.7.75: PO8 Antonio de la Fuente (Ailsa) 4.7.75: PO9 Leon Guzman (Scott) 7.4.75: P10 Ignacio Ramirez (Ailsa) 17.7.75: P11 Ignacio Mariscal (Ailsa) 23.9.75: P12 Heriberto Jara Corona (Ailsa) 7.11.75: P13 Jose Maria Maja (Lamont) 13.10.75: P14 Felix Romero (Scott) 23.6.75: P15 Fernando Lizardi (Ailsa) 24.12.75: P16 Francisco J. Mujica (Ailsa) 21.11.75: P17 Pastor Rouaix (Scott) 7.11.75: P18 Jose Maria del Castillo Velasco (Lamont) 14.1.76: P19 Luis Manuel Rojas (Lamont) 3.4.76: P20 Jose Nativadad Macias (Lamont) 2.9.76: P21 Esteban Baca Calderon (Lamont) 18.6.76: P22 Ignacio Zaragoza (Vera Cruz) 1.6.76.

Power Plant: Standard installation employs twin 3,600 bhp Paxman Ventura 12 YJCM turbo-charged marine diesels, flexibly mounted and coupled to reverse/reduction gearboxes and driving twin aluminium bronze propellers. Twin 4,800 bhp 16 YJCMs can be fitted for increased power.

Hull: All welded mild steel construction on longitudinal stringers and web frames. Superstructure in aluminium alloy. Wide beam, some 30 per cent. greater than many existing patrol boat designs of similar overall length.

Crew: Designed for complement of up to 25 officers and ratings. All accommodation and main working spaces air-conditioned.

Weapons: Single 40 mm. gun on foredeck; twin 20 mm. mounting aft and two 2 in. rocket launchers.

Dimensions: Length overall 34.1 m. (111.8 ft): beam 8.6 m. (28.1 ft): draft 2.0 m. (6.8 ft).

Displacement: 130 tons.

Performance: Maximum speed 24 knots. Range 2,500 n. miles at 12 knots.

5 **BH.7 Mk 5A Wellington**, Iran.

Six BH.7 hovercraft are operated by the Iranian Navy. Two are BH.7 Mk 4s, which are employed on logistics duties and have bow loading doors, and four are Mk 5As. These are combined combat and logistics craft, and carry medium-range surface-to-surface missiles, such as Standard SM-1 or Harpoon, on their sidedecks. A dual fast attack/logistic capability is retained by the provision of a bow door.

When employed in the coastal defence role, the main central cabin is equipped as an operation and fire control room. Communications, navigation and search and strike radar displays are installed in the operations room which is located immediately below the control cabin.

Since it is fully amphibious, the BH.7 Mk 5A can be operated from relatively unprepared bases on beaches and can head at 58 knots directly towards its target on interception missions totally regardless of the nature of the terrain and the tidal state. Another advantage is that, since none of the craft's solid structure is immersed, it is invulnerable to acoustic, magnetic and pressure mines and to torpedo attack. The craft has an endurance of up to 11 hours under cruising conditions but this can be extended substantially as it can stay on watch without employing the main engine. Radar and other navigational aids permit the BH.7 to operate both by day and by night.

BH.7s have led to the development of a new coastal defence concept which dispenses completely with the traditional concept of standing off-shore patrols. Operating in conjunction with early warning radar, they are 'scrambled' like jet fighters to intercept and interrogate suspected hostile craft by a sector controller. They can be operated from either fixed bases or a 'mother' ship patrolling off-shore. When operating from fixed bases, the craft are deployed either on concrete hardstandings above the shoreline or concealed amid dunes behind the shoreline.

In the Persian Gulf, the Imperial Iranian Navy employs a squadron of eight SR.N6 Winchesters in addition to its six BH.7s. Duties undertaken by these craft include the security of oil traffic in the Persian Gulf, the control of smuggling, support of isolated police posts and counter-insurgency operations. In 1969 the I.I.N. employed its hovercraft to occupy three strategic islands to ensure Iranian command of the Straits of Hormez.

Pennant Nos Iranian Navy BH.7s
   BH.7 002 (IIN 101) Mk 4; BH.7 003 (IIN 102) Mk 4; BH.7 004 (IIN 103) Mk 5A; BH.7 005 (IIN 104) Mk 5A; BH.7 006 (IIN 105) Mk 5A; BH.7 007 (IIN 106) Mk 5A.
Power Plant: Integrated lift and propulsion arrangement powered by a Rolls-Royce/BS Marine Proteus 15M/549 gas-turbine with a continuous output of 3,800 hp at 15°C. This drives via a shaft and bevel drive gearbox, a 12-blade, 3.5 m. (11 ft 6 in.) diameter centrifugal fan and a 6.40 m. (21 ft) diameter, variable-pitch, pylon-mounted propeller.
Hull: Fabricated mainly in corrosion resistant light alloy.
Armament: Two launchers for SM–1, Exocet or similar missiles on sidedecks, and two roof-mounted single 20 mm. cannon.
Crew Accommodation: Control cabin accommodates three crew members: driver, navigator/radar operator and third member. Additional crew according to operations room and fire control system requirements. Control cabin air-conditioned, rest areas air-conditioned and sound-proofed.
Dimensions: Length overall, 23.9 m. (78 ft 4 in.); beam 13.8 m. (45 ft 6 in.); height overall on launching pads 10.36 m. (34 ft); skirt depth 1.67 m. (5 ft 6 in.).
Weights: Normal gross weight 50 tons. Payload 14 tons.
Performance: Maximum speed over calm water, 60 knots. Average speed in 1.37 m. (4 ft 6 in.) seas, 35.5 knots.

6 **Babochka**, U.S.S.R.
One of the latest additions to Russia's sea defences, Babochka is the biggest and most powerful hydrofoil patrol boat in service today. Designed for anti-submarine warfare on open seas, it carries eight ASW torpedoes and two quadruple

mounts immediately ahead of the deckhouse. When foilborne power is supplied by three marinized gas-turbines, each with a maximum output of 25,000 shp.

Power Plant: Three marinized gas-turbines, each rated at 25,000 shp maximum. If propeller-driven either Vee or Z-drive are likely to be employed so as to provide as great a clearance height as possible.

Foil System: Probably of conventional surface-piercing Vee configuration, with an automatic control system (ACS) operating trailing edge flaps on each foil.

Armament: Two 30 mm. L/65 twin mounts for AA defence activated by a Bass Tilt fire-control radar. Six ASW torpedo tubes in two triple mounts ahead of deckhouse. Electronic equipment includes High Pole B IFF and Square Head and Peel Cone radar.

Dimensions: Length overall 50 m.

Displacement: Fully loaded, about 400 tons.

Performance: Max. speed foilborne, 50 knots plus.

7 **CPIC**, South Korea.

The CPIC (Coastal Patrol Interdiction Craft) is the only displacement vessel described in these pages employing waterjet propulsion. Conceived by the U.S. Navy during the final phase of the Vietnam War, it was intended as a replacement for the 50 ft Swift class vessels employed for the interception and clearance of junks and other light vessels inshore which might have been carrying supplies to units of the Viet Cong. One of the chief advantages of equipping the craft with waterjets is that its draught could be reduced, permitting it to operate closer inshore than other craft of similar displacement. Since it is larger than the Swift, it can also operate in higher sea states. Stabilizing fins are fitted to enhance its stability in bad weather. The lead craft, built by the Tacoma Boatbuilding Co., Tacoma, Washington, was completed in 1974 and after a lengthy evaluation by the U.S. Navy, was transferred to South Korea in August 1975.

Power Plant: Three Avco Lycoming TF 25 marinized gas-turbines, each rated at 1,800 shp, and each driving a waterjet propulsion unit. Two 250 bhp Volvo diesels power outboard drive propellers for cruising and manoeuvring.

Crew: Officers and ratings, eleven.

Armament: Two twin 30 mm. Emerlec gun mounts, one forward, one amidships. Missile launchers can be fitted on the aft deck. Light machine-guns can be fitted on the deck amidships, port and starboard.

Fire Control: Special system evolved by Honeywell for this craft under the U.S. Navy's CPIC programme. Known as the Radar Gun Fire Control System (RGFCS) Ex 93, it is designed primarily for the engagement of surface craft, but can be employed against spotter and similar aircraft. The system incorporates a navigation capability and can also be used for area surveillance and the analysis of surface traffic.

Dimensions: Length overall, 30.5 m. (100 ft): beam 5.6 m. (18.5 ft): draught 1.8 m. (6 ft).

Displacement: Fully loaded 71.25 tons.

Performance: Maximum speed, waterjet propulsion, about 45 knots.

8 **Combattante I, II and III**, France.

Development of this outstandingly successful series of diesel-powered patrol boats began in 1960 when the French navy ordered the 42 m. wooden-hulled La Combattante fast patrol boat as a test platform for early generation anti-ship missiles. The vessel, which was capable of 23 knots, entered service in 1964 and was employed initially in the evaluation of naval variants of the SS-11 and 12 wire-guided, anti-tank missiles. Later, in 1970, a single Exocet launcher was fitted as part of a crash programme to develop a missile to counter the threat of the Soviet Styx anti-ship missile.

Apart from its role in helping to perfect the Exocet, La Combattante had little influence on the design of subsequent members of the series.

Combattante II had its origins in the mid-1960s when Israeli military planners, ever-alert to any threats to national survival, recognized the need to develop a sea-skimming missile system, later to be called the Gabriel, to counter the Styx-equipped Komars and Osas transferred to Egypt and Syria by the Soviet Union. No Western anti-ship missile existed at the time! Exocet was the first to be developed by a Western nation. It was the Israeli navy's intention to mount the Gabriels on six 45 m. fast attack craft, which were to be ordered from Lürssen Werft of Bremen-Vegesack in 1945. On learning that the Israelis planned to replace the torpedo tubes of the Lürssen boats with missiles the West German Government at once refused to allow the order to be accepted for fear of upsetting the relations with the Arab states. However, the Lürssen yard was permitted to pass on its designs to Constructions Mécaniques de Normandie (CMN). Between 1965 and 1969 CMN built twelve of these craft which became known as the Saar class. (Page 145.)

In 1970 CMN 'stretched' the Lürssen design by 2 m., equipped it with four Exocets, and offered it on the export market as the Combattante II. The first customer was the navy of the German Federal Republic which urgently needed missile-equipped fast attack craft to patrol the exit to the Baltic and had no anti-ship missiles of its own. As a result, twenty Combattante IIs, known in Western Germany as the Type 148, were commissioned between October 1972 and August 1975. Eight of the steel hulls were constructed by Lürssen but all were fitted out in France. Orders were later placed by Greece (Ipopliarchos Anninos class); Malaysia (Perdana class) and Iran (Kaman class).

In May 1973, four Combattante IIs were delivered to the Malaysian navy under their own power. Averaging 20 knots for the 13,000 mile passage, they arrived in what was described as 'a fully operational condition', despite having encountered sea states 4–7 for almost one-third of the journey.

Initially Combattante IIs were fitted with four MM38 Exocet anti-ship missile launchers. These have now been replaced in some variants by four Harpoon launchers.

Combattante II
Power Plant: Four MTU diesels, each rated at either 4,500 or 5,000 bhp and coupled through reverse/reduction gears to four shafts fitted with three-bladed fixed-pitch propellers.
Hull: Main hull in all-welded, prefabricated steel. Aluminium superstructure.
Complement/Accommodation: Crew 30–32, four officers and 26–28 men. All living and operating spaces air-conditioned.
Armament: Original series had one 57 mm. dual-purpose gun forward and a twin 35 mm. dual-purpose mounting aft, or two twin 35 mm. mountings. In 1973 this was modified to one 76 mm. dual-purpose gun forward and one twin 35 mm. dual-purpose mounting aft. At the same time the torpedo-tubes were replaced by minelaying chutes and four Exocet missiles. A further series was introduced in late 1976 in which the Exocets were replaced by four American-built McDonnell Douglas Harpoons and Hollandse Signaalapparaten radar and weapons control system.
Dimensions: Length overall 47 m. (154 ft 2½ in.): beam 7 m. (23 ft): draught 1.90 m. (6 ft 2¾ in.).
Displacement: Average load 285 tonnes; fully loaded 311 tonnes.
Performance: Maximum speed about 37 knots, radius of action 1,600 n. miles at 15 knots.

Combattante IIG
At present this exists as a project only. Some 2.20 m. longer than Combattante II it would be powered by four 4,500 bhp MTU Type 20V-538-TB91 diesels. A twin 40 mm. Bofors/Breda AA gun would be mounted aft and a Vega II fire control system would be installed.

Dimensions: Length overall 49 m. (160 ft 9 in.): beam 7.60 m. (25 ft): draught 2.20 m. (7 ft 2½ in.).
Displacement: Standard 260 tonnes, fully loaded 311 tonnes.
Performance: Maximum speed 39 knots, endurance 1,600 n. miles at 15 knots.

Combattante III
Most lethal member of the series is the Combattante III, four of which have been supplied to the Greek navy. The hull has undergone a 9 m. stretch in order to provide deck space for a second 76 mm. dual-purpose cannon and two 21 in. wire-guided torpedo tubes aft and two twin 30 mm. Emerlec light AA mountings amidships.
Power Plant: Four MTU 20V-538-TB91 diesels, each rated at 4,500 hp maximum and 3,750 cruising and coupled via reverse/reduction gearboxes to four shafts, each fitted with a three-bladed fixed-pitch propeller.
Hull: Main hull in all-welded, prefabricated steel. Aluminium superstructure. Flush decked.
Complement/Accommodation: Crew, 42 officers and men. All living and operating spaces air-conditioned. Two independent plants.
Armament: Two 76 mm. dual-purpose cannon, one forward, one aft. Two twin 30 mm. Emerlec AA cannon amidships, port and starboard. Two 21 in. wire-guided torpedoes and four missile launchers (either Exocets with Thomson-CSF Vega fire control system or Harpoons with Hollandse Signaalapparaten radar and fire control system). All weapons can be operated effectively at up to sea state 6.
Dimensions: Length overall 56.15 m. (184 ft 2¾ in.): beam 8 m. (26 ft 3 in.): depth 4.40 m. (14 ft 5¼ in.): draught 2.40 m. (7 ft 10½ in.).
Displacement: Average load, 392 tonnes, full load 425 tonnes.
Performance: Maximum speed 35 knots. Endurance 2,000 n. miles at 15 knots.

9 **Constitución**, Venezuela.

Six of these 37 m. steel-hulled fast patrol boats were completed by Vosper-Thornycroft for the Venezuelan navy between 1974–75. The craft were ordered as replacements for a mixed force of ageing ex-British and American destroyers. In making their choice the Venezuelans were influenced by two major considerations: the very high cost of warships in the 1–2,000 ton bracket and the ability of today's small surface strike vessels to engage much larger ships in battle as well as defend themselves against aircraft and guided missiles.

The length of 37 m. was selected as it is the smallest size that can comfortably accommodate a modern 76 mm. automatic cannon and its associated fire control radar as well as mount long-range anti-ship missiles such as Exocet, Otomat or Seakiller. The hull, which is all-welded steel with an aluminium alloy superstructure, is derived from that of the Tenacity. Deep vee sections are provided forward for good seakeeping followed by a round bilge. A spray strake runs round more than half the length of the vessel to keep the upper deck as dry as possible. Stabilizing fins are fitted.

Three of the Constitución class are equipped with Oto Melara 76 mm. 62 cal. rapid fire cannon and three with two Otomat Mk 2 missile launchers aft and a 40 mm. gun forward.

Class Names/Launch Dates
P11, Constitución, 1.6.73: P12, Federación, 26.2.74: P13, Independencia, 24.7.73: P14, Libertad, 5.3.74: P15, Patria, 27.9.73: P16, Victoria, 3.9.74.

Power Plant: Twin MTU 16-cylinder Type MD 16V 538TB90 diesels, each with a maximum continuous rating of 2,950 bhp at 1,790 rpm and a sprint rating of 3,540 bhp at 1,900 rpm. Each engine drives a Monel K-500 propeller via an MTU reverse reduction gearbox.

Accommodation: Air-conditioned living and working spaces. Crew comprises four officers, four petty officers and ten ratings.
Armament: Missile-equipped vessels (Federación, Libertad and Victoria): Two Otomat Mk 2 anti-ship missiles and one 40 mm. gun forward. Gun-only vessels (Constitución, Independencia and Patria): One 76 mm. Oto Melara 76/62 automatic gun forward.
Dimensions: Length overall 36.88 m. (121 ft); moulded beam 7.16 m. (23.4 ft): draught 1.73 m. (5.7 ft).
Displacement: 150 tons.
Performance: Max. speed 31 knots.
Range: 1,350 n. miles at 16 knots,
Radar/Fire Control: The 76/72 cannon is controlled by an Elettronica San Giorgio (ELSAG) NA10 Mod O fire control system.

10 **Dabur (Hornet)**, Israel.

This diesel-powered 35-ton coastal patrol vessel is an enlarged version of the boats built in the United States by Swiftships Inc. of New Orleans to service offshore drilling rigs in the Caribbean. The first military derivative, bristling with machine-guns and grenade launchers, was employed on coastal patrol and interdiction duties by the U.S. Navy's Coastal Surveillance Force in Vietnam. Subsequently, the Israeli Navy ordered an enlarged, 65 ft model, the Dabur, the first twelve of which were built in New Orleans. Since March 1975 a further eighteen have been built by the Ramta Systems & Structures Plant of Israel Aircraft Industries, Beersheba, Israel.

Primary application of the Dabur has been anti-infiltration patrol along Israel's Mediterranean and Red Sea coasts, although the American-built craft were also employed in raids on Red Sea harbours during the 1973 'Yom Kippur' war. The Dabur carries a crew of six and mounts two 20 mm.

cannon. Radar-equipped, it has a maximum draught of only 1.75 m. (5 ft 9 in.) and a top speed of 22 knots.

Crews speak highly of the craft which has excellent seakeeping characteristics, especially in long swells, and the ability to operate in sea state 4.

Power Plant: Two 480 hp General Motors Detroit Diesels 12V71 turbocharged marine diesels, each driving its own propeller shaft. Total fuel capacity, 1,800 gal.
Hull: Welded all-aluminium main structure.
Complement/Accommodation: Crew 6. Air conditioning system provided for crew, galley and pilothouse.
Armament: Standard arrangement comprises two 20 mm. guns – one forward, one aft – and two .50 calibre machine-guns located on the open bridge. Other types of weaponry according to requirements. Torpedo tubes have been fitted forward.
Dimensions: Length overall 19.75 m. (64 ft 11 in.): beam 5.49 m. (18 ft): draught max. 1.75 m. (5 ft 9 in.).
Displacement: Fully loaded, 35 tons.
Performance: Cruising at 2,100 rpm, 19.6 knots; max. rpm 21.8 knots.
Range: 1,295 km. (700 n. miles).
Endurance: Patrol endurance reported to be up to 48 hours, although missions rarely extend beyond 24 hours' duration.
Radio and Navigation Systems: British-built surveillance radar and Israeli-made communications equipment.

11 **Nasty,** Turkey.
The Nasty class fast patrol boat was designed by Båtservis Mandal, Norway, in the early 1960s and variants were subsequently supplied to the U.S., West German, Greek, Norwegian and Turkish navies. Fourteen of these craft were built

in Norway for the U.S. Navy between 1962 and 1964 and a further six craft, based on the Nasty design, were built for the U.S. Navy by John Trumpy & Sons, Annapolis, Maryland, between 1967–70. Extensive use was made of the Norwegian-built vessels in the Vietnam War for interdiction and support work and six were lost as a result of enemy action.

Torpedo-boat versions of almost identical design are in service with the Norwegian, Greek and Turkish navies. Series production of the Nasty-class is currently underway at the Taskizake Dockyard, Istanbul, Turkey. Although the torpedo has been replaced to a great extent by the guided missile, the former is still an extremely formidable weapon in narrows and areas dotted with offshore islands, a feature particularly prevalent off the coast of Turkey.

Class Names or Designations/Delivery Dates
West German Navy. Two vessels delivered by Båtservis and transferred to Turkey in 1964.
Norwegian Navy. See separate entry for Tjeld class.
Greek Navy. Pennant Numbers/Class Names (all craft commissioned during 1967). P21 Andromeda: P23 Kastor: P24 Kyknos: P25 Pigassos: P26 Toxotis.
Power Plant: Two 18-cylinder Napier Deltic Type 59K charge-air cooled turbocharged diesels, each developing 3,100 bhp and each driving its own propeller shaft.
Hull: Mixed wood and grp construction. Mahogany, fibreglass, mahogany sandwich.
Complement: Three officers, sixteen enlisted men.
Armament: U.S. Navy variants mounted one 81 mm. mortar, one .50 cal. machine-gun above over mortar, one 40 mm. rapid-fire cannon and two 20 mm. guns. Greek and Turkish Navy Craft: two single 40 mm. AA mounts and four 21 in. torpedo tubes.
Dimensions: Length overall 24.50 m. (80.3 ft): beam, 6.40 m. (21 ft): draught 2.06 m. (6.75 ft).

Displacement: Standard, 63.75 tons, fully loaded 74.5 tons.
Performance: Maximum speed, 45 knots. Endurance, 450 miles at 41 knots, or 600 miles at 25 knots.

12 **Flagstaff II**, Israel.

Early in 1966 the U.S. Navy placed contracts with Grumman Aerospace Corporation and Boeing's Marine Systems Division for two 60-ton patrol gunboat hydrofoils, the PGH-1 Flagstaff with a controllable-pitch supercavitating propeller employing a Z-drive and the PGH-2 Tucumcari, propelled by waterjets. The craft were built to an operational requirement which grew out of the need for high-performance gunboats at the time of the Cuban missile crisis. Both craft underwent combat evaluation as part of the U.S. Navy's Vietnam coastal surveillance force between September 1969 and February 1970. This exercise showed that both craft could operate in sea-states twice that required in their design specifications and that, because of their smoother ride, maintenance was lower than that of comparable conventional vessels.

In October 1976, the Flagstaff I was transferred permanently to the U.S. Coast Guard and recommissioned as a U.S.C.G. cutter. Designated WPGH-1, it is in service with Coast Guard District 1 (New England Area) where it is being employed to evaluate the use of hydrofoils for Coast Guard duties including the enforcement of laws and treaties, fisheries and contraband reinforcement and search and rescue.

In 1975 an updated and lengthened version of the PGH-1 was announced as the Flagstaff II. With a length of 25.74 m. (84 ft 5 in.) – 3.04 m. (10 ft) longer than the PGH-1 – this new variant is designed to carry a wide range of alternative military loads. Foilborne power is supplied by either an Allison 501KF or a Rolls-Royce RM-2D Tyne marine gas-turbine. In the early autumn of 1977 it was announced by the U.S. Government that agreement had been reached on the joint development of hydrofoils by the two countries and Grumman revealed that it had 'received its first order for the Flagstaff from Israel'. Construction will also be undertaken by Israel Shipyards Ltd, Haifa, which builds the 415 ton Reshef (Flash) fast attack missilecraft for the Israeli and overseas navies.

Foil System: Fully submerged, incidence-controlled system of 'aeroplane' configuration consisting of twin inverted T foils forward and a single inverted T foil aft. The stern foil/power strut, together with the foilborne propeller, rotates ± 5 degrees for steering and all three foil/strut units retract clear of the water for shallow draft operations and hullborne manoeuvring on harbour.
Hull: All-welded aluminium structure.
Crew: Depending on duties. Minimum 7–8. Nominal complement, fifteen.
Power Plant: (Foilborne). Choice of either a 3,980 bhp (continuous) Allison 501KF or a 4,680 bhp (continuous) Rolls-Royce RM2D marine Tyne. Power is transmitted to a controllable-pitch, supercavitating propeller via a Z-drive transmission. *(Hullborne power.)* Twin 216 hp GM 6V53N diesels driving either retractable outdrives or waterjet pumps, depending on operator's preference.
Armament: Missiles: Either Harpoon, Gabriel, Otomat, Exocet or Penguin type. Guns: One or two 30 mm. or 40 mm. gun mounts.
Dimensions: Length overall 25.74 m. (84 ft 5 in.): beam overall, foilborne 29.81 m. (97 ft 10 in.): draught, foilborne 1.7 m. (5 ft 7 in.): hullborne foils retracted, 1.45 m. (4 ft 9 in.).
Weights: Light displacement, 59.8 tonnes: fully loaded 92 tonnes.
Performance: Maximum intermittent speed, 52 knots: normal foilborne operating speed range, 35–48 knots.

13 Freccia, Italy.

Built by Cantiere Navali Liguri di Riva Trigoso SpA, Freccia is a highly versatile medium-size fast attack craft which can be converted within a single day to operate in the following roles: gunboat, fast minelayer, missilecraft or torpedo boat. The success of the Freccia has led to the basic design being adopted for more recent concepts, including the CNR-280, which mounts a 76 mm. Oto Melara dual-purpose cannon and four Otomat missiles.

Its sister craft, the Saetta, built by CRDA of Monfalcone, has been armed with Sistel Sea Killer Mk I, beam-riding sea skimmer missiles which are launched from five-round multiple launchers.

Pennant Numbers/Class Names/Year of Commissioning
P493 Freccia (1965): P494 Saetta (1966):
Power Plant: Single 4,250 shp Rolls-Royce Marine Proteus gas-turbine for sprint performance. Two 3,800 bhp diesels for cruising.
Crew: Four officers and thirty-three men.
Armament: Equipped as missilecraft. One or more multiple launchers for Sea Killer missiles. Gunboat configuration: three 40 mm. cannon: Torpedo-boat configuration: two 21 in. torpedoes and two 40 mm. cannon: fast minelayer configuration: eight mines and one 40 mm. cannon.
Dimensions: Length 45.8 m. (150 ft): beam 7.3 m. (23.8 ft): draft 1.7 m. (5.5 ft).
Displacement: Standard 188 tons, fully loaded, 205 tons.
Performance: Sprint speed in excess of 40 knots.

14 Guacolda, Chile.

This 36 m. fast attack torpedo craft is one of four built by Lürssen's Spanish Licence, Empresa Nacional Bazan, for the Chilean navy during 1965–66. Similar outwardly to the Manta class vessels built by Lürssen for Ecuador, it differs mainly in installed power. Craft of the Guacolda class are fitted with two 2,400 bhp MTU diesels, while those of the Manta class have three 3,000 bhp diesels.

Power Plant: Two 2,400 bhp MTU diesels, each driving its own propeller shaft.
Complement: Twenty officers and men.
Armament: Two 40 mm. Bofors AA guns, and four 21 in. Torpedo-tubes.
Dimensions: Length overall 36 m.: beam 5.6 m.: draught 2.2 m.
Weights: Displacement, fully loaded, 134 tons.
Performance: Max. speed 32 knots. Range 1,500 n. miles at 15 knots.

15 **Hauk**, Norway.

The Royal Norwegian Navy's new Hauk class missilecraft is similar in external appearance and overall dimensions to the earlier Snögg class. Fourteen were ordered in June 1975 as part of a large naval re-equipment programme, the first being officially delivered on 5 August 1977. Like the metal-hulled Snögg class, the primary armament comprises four Penguin guided missiles, although these are of a longer range than the earlier 1970 models and have been developed in conjunction with the Royal Swedish Navy which is employing similar missiles on its new Hugin class. Another feature of the Hauk is the adoption of improved combat information and weapons control systems. Ten units of the Hauk class are being built by Bergens Mekaniske Verksteder and four by Westermöen.

Pennant Numbers:
 P986 to P999.
Power Plant: Two 3,500 hp MTU diesels, each driving its own propeller shaft.
Hull: Welded steel construction.

Crew: Officers and ratings, 22.
Armament: Missiles: four Penguin; Torpedoes; four 21 in.: Guns; one 40 mm. Bofors 40/70.
Electronics: Weapon control system, Kongsberg Vapenfabrikk MSI-80s.
Dimensions: Length overall 36.5 m. (119.7 ft): beam 6.2 m. (20.34 ft): draft 1.6 m. (5.25 ft).
Weights: Average load, 120 tons, full load, 150 tons.
Performance: Cruising speed 34 knots. Range at cruising speed 440 miles.

16 **Hu Chwan (White Swan)**, China.

Fast attack torpedo hydrofoils of the Hu Chwan class have been under construction at the Hutang Shipyard, Hong Kong since 1966. About 120 are in service with the navy of the Chinese People's Republic, another thirty-two are operating in the Adriatic with the Albanian Navy, six have been supplied to Pakistan and three to Romania. A further six, with heavier armament have been built in Romania.

In much the same way as the earlier Soviet P8, the Hu Chwan is based on an earlier displacement torpedo-boat hull to which a bow foil has been added for increased performance in relatively calm conditions. The foil system comprises a bow subfoil to facilitate take-off and a trapeze or shallow V main foil set back approximately one-third of the hull length from the bow. At high speed all but the stern of the hull is raised clear of the water.

Power Plant: Three 1,200 hp M.50 watercooled, supercharged 12-cylinder V-type diesels each driving its own propeller shaft.
Hull: V-bottom, light-alloy hull.
Armament: Two 21 in. torpedo tubes, plus four 12.7 in. machine-guns in two twin mountings.
Dimensions: Length overall 21.33 m. (70 ft): width overall 5.02 m. (16 ft 6 in.): hull beam 3.96 m. (13 ft).

Weights: Displacement, full load 45 tons.
Performance: Max. speed foilborne calm conditions, 55 knots. Range, 500 n. miles.

17 **Hugin**, Sweden.
Fast attack craft are considered invaluable for the protection of countries with long serrated coastlines, particularly where the immediate offshore area is rich in islands. Inlets provide the FAC with opportunities to lie in ambush while narrows and straits place larger marauding craft at an immediate disadvantage because of the navigational hazards. Such a country is Sweden, where the coast is 2,700 km. long and stretches from the northernmost point of the Baltic to southern Norway. Stockholm, its capital, is separated from the sea, nearly 48 km. away, by the Stockholm archipelago, which alone consists of 10,000 wooded islands and islets. The defence of such an area from a seaborne assault requires a very large number of small, fast attack craft. Fortunately, it is now possible to build small and relatively inexpensive ships capable of combating even the heaviest of warships on almost equal terms. In the event of a conflict the Royal Swedish Navy would employ a fleet of submarines, missile boats and torpedo boats, operating in conjunction with strike aircraft, to attack an approaching invasion fleet.

One of Sweden's latest fast attack craft is the 140 ton Hugin missile gunboat, similar in overall design and construction to the Royal Norwegian Navy's Hauk.

One of the main features of this class is the installation of a fully integrated and automated missile and gun weapon-control system, built by Philips Elektronikindustrier AB (PEAB) and designated 9LV200 Mk 2. Employing only three operators this controls one or more guns against the same or different aircraft or surface targets, and will engage surface targets simultaneously with missiles.

The high accuracy of the system has been verified by many

test firings at sea. When using proximity fuze ammunition in the Bofors L70 dual-purpose gun against high speed towed targets, a salvo of two or three rounds generally destroys the target at a range of 2–3 km., even in rough seas. The normal time lapse between the first detection of a target and the opening of fire with full accuracy is between 5–10 seconds.

Like the Hauk, the Hugin is being built in Norway. In May 1975, an order for eleven was placed with Bergens Mekaniske Verksted and five from Westermöen. The prototype and first two series production craft are in service. Production is not expected to be complete until 1982.

Pennant Nos:
P150–166.
Power Plant: Two MTU MB20V 672 TY90 marine diesels, each delivering 3,500 bhp.
Hull: Welded steel.
Crew: Officers and ratings, 20.
Armament: Missiles: Six Penguin Mk 2 missiles. Guns: One 57 mm. Bofors L70 dual-purpose cannon. Provision for second gun mounting aft of deckhouse.
Torpedo Tubes: Can be equipped with four 21 in. (533 mm.) torpedoes. Also provision for minelaying.
Electronics: PEAB 9LV200 Mk 2 weapon control system.
Dimensions: Length overall 36 m. (118 ft): beam 6.2 m. (20.3 ft): draft 1.5 m. (4.9 ft).
Displacement: Fully loaded, 140 tons.
Performance: Cruising speed, 35 knots.

18 **Jaguar**, German Federal Republic.
Lürssen Werft, one of the world's oldest independent shipbuilders, celebrated its centenary in 1975. Since its earliest days it had specialized in racing boats, seagoing motor cruisers, rescue craft and fast ferries. A working partnership with the Daimler engine company, now part of MTU, was estab-

lished as far back as 1890. Lürssen's first torpedo-boats were active in World War I in the Baltic and off the coast of Flanders. During World War II the company's yard at Vegesack was engaged exclusively in the construction of motor torpedo-boats for the German Navy. It employed a workforce of 1,000 and at the peak of its war-time activity is reported to have completed a new vessel every six days. Certainly, by 1945 it had constructed a total of 167 MTBs, 14 minesweepers and many smaller craft.

Lürssen's first major post war order for torpedo-boats was placed by the Royal Swedish Navy in 1954. This was for eleven units of the 170 ton Plejad class, round-bilge vessels powered by three 3,000 bhp diesels and capable of 37.5 knots. When the West German Navy was re-established in 1955, it contracted Lürssen to build a similar design which became known as the Type 140–141 Jaguar class. Thirty-two of these craft were built by Lürssen between 1957 and 1962 and eight by Kröger of Rendsburg, between 1958 and 1964. Nine of the nineteen Jaguar class vessels which actually entered service with the West German Navy were fitted with Mercedes-Benz 20-cylinder diesel engines and were known as the Type 140, and the remaining ten were equipped with Maybach 16-cylinder diesels and known as the Type 141. Ten craft originally built to the Jaguar class design were later converted into the Type 142 Zobel class.

Jaguars of the West German Navy were paid off in 1975, but a number of units have been transferred to or built for overseas navies including Ecuador, Ghana and Turkey. The ten Zobel fast attack torpedo craft are still fully operational.

Power Plant: Four 3,000 shp MTU16V538 or Maybach diesels, each driving a fixed-pitch propeller.
Hull: Composite, transverse-framed construction. Frames, bulkheads and deck beams in welded light alloy. Triple thickness, diagonally bonded mahogany outer skin bolted to alloy ribs.

Complement: Thirty-nine officers and men.
Armament: Two 40 mm. Bofors L70 anti-aircraft guns, one forward, one aft. Two 21 in. torpedo tubes or alternatively rails for four mines.
Dimensions: Length overall 42.5 m. (139.4 ft), beam 7.2 m. (23.4 ft): draught 7.9 m. (2.4 ft).
Weights: Loaded displacement, 190 tons, standard 160 tons.
Performance: Maximum speed 42 knots.

Jaguar II & III
In August 1977, it was announced that Lürssen had been awarded an order for four fast missile boats for Ghana. Two are of the new 45 m. long, 250 ton Type 45 Jaguar II design and the other two of the enlarged 58 m. long, 400 ton Type 57 Jaguar III design. Both variants mount Oto Melara 76/62 dual-purpose rapid-firing cannon and are equipped with the Thomson-CSF Vega fire-control system. Both are armed with MM 38 Exocet anti-ship missiles.

19 **Isku,** Finland.
Isku is a training craft for the crews of Osa fast attack missile-craft ordered from the Soviet Union by the Finnish Navy. Nine craft are on order and each is to be fitted with Finnish designed surveillance and fine control systems. Built at the Reposaaron Konepaja Yard and launched in late 1969, the vessel is based on a flat-bottomed landing craft hull.

Power Plant: Four Soviet-built M-50 12-cylinder four-stroke, water-cooled diesels, each with a normal output of 1,000 hp and each driving its own propeller shaft.
Dimensions: Length overall 26 m. (85.30 ft); beam 8.7 m. (28.54 ft); draught 1.8 m. (5.91 ft).
Displacement: Fully loaded, 140 tons.
Performance: Max. speed, about 25 knots.

20 **Kartal**, Turkey.

Nine Jaguar type fast attack torpedo craft were built by Lürssen for the Turkish Navy between 1966–1968 and became known as the Kartal class. In 1975 four of these, the Albatross, Meltem, Pelikan and Simsek were re-armed with Harpoon anti-ship missiles.

During 1975 seven ex-West German Navy Jaguar-class torpedo-boats were transferred to Turkey. Three further craft were supplies for cannibalization to supply spare parts. A description of the Jaguar appears on page 120.

Pennant Nos/Class Names/Commissioning Dates

P327 Albatros, 1968: P322 Atmaca 1967: P321 Denizkusu 1967: P324 Kartal 1967: P329 Kasirga 1967: P325 Meltem 1968: P326 Pelikan 1968: P323 Sahin 1967: P328 Simsek 1968.

21 **Kris**, Malaysia.

Employed by the Malaysia Navy for coastal patrol, fishery protection and contraband control, the Kris class is based on Vosper Thornycroft's 31.3 m. (102 ft) standard FPM design. Armed with two 40 mm. Bofors cannon and fitted with Vosper stabilizers it is said to be the smallest patrol boat capable of maintaining a speed of 25 knots in normal conditions in the open sea. Fourteen vessels of this type were supplied to Malaysia between December 1966 and February 1968.

Pennant Nos/Class Name/Commissioning Date:

P37 Badek, 15.12.66: P44 Beledau, 12.9.67: P45 Kelewang 4.10.67: P43 Kerambit, 28.7.67: P34 Kris 1.1.66: P40 Lembing 12.4.67: P42 Panah 27.7.67: P38 Renchong, 17.1.67: P46 Rentaka, 22.9.67: P41 Serampang, 19.5.67: P49 Sri Johor, 14.2.68: P47 Sri Perlis, 24.1.68: P36 Sundang, 29.11.66: P39 Tombak, 2.3.67.

Power Plant: Two 1,750 hp MTU MD 655/18 or Paxman 12 YJCM 12-cylinder diesels, each driving its own propeller shaft.

Hull: Prefabricated construction in all-welded mild steel. Superstructure in aluminium alloy.

Crew: Normal crew comprises captain, two officers, three petty officers and sixteen junior ratings. All interior spaces air-conditioned apart from engine rooms,

Armament: Two 40 mm. Bofors cannon with 1,000 rounds of ammunition, two rocket flare launchers with 44 flares, plus small arms.

Dimensions: Length overall 31.25 m. (102 ft 6½ in.); max. beam 6.02 m. (19 ft 9 in.); draught aft (deep) 1.98 m. (6 ft 6 in.).

Performance: Maximum speed, temperate climate, 27 knots. Maximum continuous speed, 25.5 knots. Cruising range, 1,800 n. miles at 14 knots.

22 **Komar (Mosquito)**, Algeria.

A foretaste of the effect that missile-equipped fast attack craft would have on naval warfare in the future was the sinking of the Israeli destroyer Eilat, 13 miles off Port Said, on 21 October 1967 by four Styx missiles launched by Komars of the Egyptian Navy moored within Port Said Harbour.

Credit for the idea of marrying the guided missiles to the fast patrol boat hull is generally attributed to Sergey Georgievich Gorshkov, Soviet Admiral of the Fleet. Realizing that the Soviet Navy was totally incapable of competing with the air power of a U.S. Navy task force at sea, he set out to devise a quick and inexpensive threat to American aircraft carriers. The answer was the Komar, derived from the wooden-hulled P.6-class torpedo-boats, and equipped with two SS-N-2A 'Styx' missile launchers, one each side of the aft superstructure.

The first Komars entered service in 1961. By 1974 some 25 had been delivered to the Soviet Navy and another 118 had been transferred to overseas navies as follows: Algeria 6, China 60, Cuba 18, Egypt 4, Indonesia 12, North Korea 10, Syria 6 and Vietnam 2.

Between 1975–6 eight Komars were built in the Egyptian Navy's shipyard at Alexandria and were named the October class, in commemoration of the Israel War in October 1973. Six of these craft are being refitted and updated by Vosper Thornycroft at Portsea at a rate of two a year. According to unconfirmed reports the craft are being modified to launch Otomat anti-ship missiles which will be operated by a Marconi-Sperry Sapphire fire control system.

Power Plant: Four 1,200 hp water-cooled, supercharged V-type diesels, each driving its own propeller shaft.
Hull: Wooden construction.
Armament: Two SS-N-2 Styx missiles. Speed about Mach 0.9; maximum range about 20 n. miles (40 km.). Single 25 mm. twin AA mounting forward.
Dimensions: Length overall 27.4 m. (83.7 ft): beam 6.5 m. (19 ft 8 in.): draft 1.6 m. (5 ft 0 in.)
Weights: Displacement, full load 80 tons; standard base weight 70 tons.
Performance: Maximum speed, calm conditions, about 40 knots; range 400 n. miles at 30 knots.

23 **Mol**, Soviet Union.
This new Soviet torpedo-boat is evidently intended to replace the ageing Shershen (Hornet), a derivative of the Osa missilecraft. Shershen, which made its debut in the early 1960s, was the Soviet Navy's first torpedo-boat designed for operation on the open seas. Mol, a more powerful and better equipped derivative, was first sighted in 1975. One has been transferred to Sri Lanka and another four to Somalia.

Although bearing a strong similarity to the Shershen class, Mol has several major distinguishing features. The bridge is almost identical to that of Turya, the deckhouse superstructure has multiple vertical stiffening ribs and the aft twin 30 mm. L/65 AA turret is sited right at the stern.

Power Plant: Thought to be three 4,000 bhp M-504 diesels, each driving its own propeller shaft.
Hull: Steel hull, aluminium superstructure.
Armament: Four 21 in. torpedoes; two twin L/65 30 mm. AA mounts.
Electronics: Pot Drum radar atop forward lattice mast with High Pole on upper rear support and Square Head antenna on console beneath, Drum Tilt control system for AA guns in aft tower.
Dimensions: Length overall 39.9 m.: beam 7.6 m.: draft 1.8 m.
Displacement: Standard, 170 tonnes; operational, 210 tonnes.
Performance: Maximum speed, 40 knots.

24 **Nanushka,** Soviet Union.
Described by the Soviet Navy as a 'missile cutter' Nanushka is the third and largest member of Admiral Serge Georgievich Gorshkov's 'giant killer' family which began with the Komar and Osa. Like its two predecessors, Nanushka is intended primarily to intercept carrier task forces approaching the Soviet coastline, although units are occasionally deployed in the Mediterranean and North Sea.

Nanushka is in series production at a rate of about three a year at the Admiralty Shipyards, Leningrad. By mid-1977 seventeen were in service with the Soviet Navy and three more with the Indian Navy. A further three were ordered by India in 1978.

Dominating visual characteristics are the huge 'thimble' dome containing the air search radar atop the bridge superstructure and the two triple cigar case missile launcher bins abreast of the deckhouse forward. One of the weaponry novelties installed on the Nanushka is the SA-N-4 surface-to-air missile system which employs a fully automatic, retractable twin launcher. Intended apparently for a close-in air defence role, the SA-N-4 operates in association with a fire-control radar system code-named Pop Group.

Power Plant: Six marine diesels, each developing 4,679 hp and coupled to drive three propeller shafts.
Hull: Steel.
Crew: 70.
Armament: Six SS-N-9s anti-ship missiles. Normal range 40 n. miles (75 km.), but could possibly be extended to 150 n. miles (275 km.) with mid-course guidance by aircraft or helicopters. SA-N-4 AA missile system forward, one twin 57 mm. automatic AA gun mounting aft. Indian Nanushkas equipped with four container launchers for SS-N-2s.
Radar and Fire Control: SS-N-9s are activated by Band Stand radar, SA-N-4 launcher is controlled by Pop Group radar and the twin 57 mm. cannon has a Muff Cob fire control radar.
Dimensions: Length overall 59 m. (193.5 ft): beam 12 m. (39.6 ft): draft 3.0 m. (9.9 ft).
Weights: Displacement, fully loaded 950 tons, standard 800 tons.
Performance: Maximum speed, 32 knots.

25 **Lance,** Senegal.

Built by Fairey Marine Limited, this craft is designed for use by police and customs authorities as either a fast patrol boat or a fast gunboat. In the latter configuration a 20 mm. cannon is mounted aft of the superstructure. Intended for general patrol duties which do not require a very high turn of speed, its hull is designed to provide a stable performance in the 10–20 knot speed range in seas in which a planing hull craft might encounter difficulties.

Power Plant: Two 425 hp GM 8V71TI diesels, each driving a standard fixed-pitch propeller. Integral fuel tanks with total capacity of 2,273 litres.

Hull: Fast patrol boat model: hull and superstructure, moulded grp. Fast gunboat version: aluminium superstructure, moulded grp hull.

Crew/Accommodation: FGB has berths for 6 plus seating for boarding party in aft compartment. All living space air-conditioned.

Armament: FGB version. Single 20 mm. cannon aft of superstructure: light machine-guns on bridge wings and foredeck. FPB version. Two light machine-guns, one forward, one aft.

Dimensions: FGB. Length overall 14.81 m.: beam 4.65 m.: draught maximum 1.30 m.: FPB Length overall 14.84 m.: beam 4.68 m.: draught maximum 1.32 m.

Weights: Trials displacement, half fuel and water: FGB, 15.7 tons, FPB 16 tons.

Performance: Maximum speed 25 knots; maximum intermittent speed 23 knots; maximum continuous speed 20 knots. Range FGB, 500 n. miles; FPB, 230 n. miles. Maximum permissible sea state or conditions, Force 6–7. Craft is currently in service with the Gambian Police (FGB), the Senegal Customs Authority (FPB) and the Army of the United Kingdom as a range safety launch.

25 **Sword.**

The prototype of this 13.7 m. long derivative of the Fairey Marine Spear fast patrol boat was launched in April 1977. Like its predecessor it features a deep vee hull built in moulded grp. Intended for use by police and customs authorities as a high speed interception craft, the standard model has a top speed of 27 knots.

Power Plant: Two 425 hp GM8V 71TI marine diesels, each driving a fixed-pitch propeller. Alternative high-speed variant available fitted with twin GM8V 92TI engines and

capable of 33 knots. Bottom and two aft tanks provide total fuel capacity of 3,182 litres.
Hull: Moulded grp main hull and superstructure.
Accommodation/Complement: Air-conditioned living spaces. Crew 6–8 officers and men.
Communications and Navigation Systems: Craft equipped to customer's requirements.
Armament: Heavy machine-gun forward, light machine-gun aft.
Dimensions: Length overall 13.7 m.: beam overall 4.10 m.: draught 1.32 m.
Weights: Light displacement, 15 tons.
Performance: Maximum speed, standard model, 28 knots. With twin GM8V 92TI marine diesels 33 knots. Range, 500 n. miles at cruising speed of 24 knots.

25 **Tracker**, United Kingdom.
This class was built originally as a high-speed rescue boat for the South African navy, to operate off the Cape of Good Hope. A variant is in service as a fast despatch vessel on the Clyde with the U.K. Ministry of Defence, while others are employed by the U.K. Customs and the Bahrain Coastguard. The current production version is the Tracker Mk 2, with enlarged wheelhouse and bridge fabricated in glass-reinforced plastics.

Power Plant: Two 645 bhp GM12V 71TI diesels, each driving a single fixed-pitch propeller. Standard double bottom tanks with capacity of 5448 l.
Hull: Moulded grp hull and superstructure.
Complement/Accommodation: Normal operating crew: eleven officers and men. All living and working spaces air-conditioned.
Armament: Two 20 mm. cannon, one forward, one aft. Light machine-gun mount on each wing of bridge.

Dimensions: Length overall 19.25 m.: beam 4.98 m.: draught 1.45 m.
Weights: Standard displacement (half fuel and water) 31.5 tonnes.
Performance: Maximum intermittent speed, 24 knots. Maximum continuous speed, 20 knots. Range, 670 n. miles at 20 knots.

25 **Spear**, Bahrain.

Employed by police and customs authorities in more than a dozen countries, this well-known grp-hulled patrol boat has a maximum intermittent speed of 29 knots and a range of 250 miles. By mid-1977 more than 100 were in service. Light machine-guns can be mounted forward and in the cockpit.

Power Plant: Two 180 hp Sabre engines, each driving its own propeller. Twin fuel tanks beneath cockpit provide total capacity of 636 litres.
Hull: Main hull and superstructure in grp.
Crew: Three.
Communications: HF SSB, VHF/UHF fitted to customers' requirements. Radar recommended; Decca 060.
Dimensions: Length overall 9.1 m. (29.8 ft); beam overall 2.89 m. (9 ft); draught maximum 0.84 m. (2.8 ft).
Displacement: 4.5 tons.
Performance: Maximum speed with twin 180 hp engines, 29 knots.

26 **Osa I and II (Wasp)**, Soviet Union.

With the introduction of Russia's Osa and Komar missile-craft, nations with small navies saw immediately that here was a lethal new addition to sea power which altered the balance of naval conflict to their advantage for the future. Small missile-firing attack craft of this type would enable them to wage a war at sea against larger and superior forces at minimum cost. The potential of these craft was proved by Osas of the Indian Navy during the war against Pakistan in 1971–1972. In an attack on shipping off Karachi on the night of 4–5 December 1971, they sank the 2,325 ton destroyer PNS Khaibar, damaged her sister craft, the Badr, and hit the Muhafiz coastal minesweeper. On the night of 8–9 December they sank one British and one Panamanian freighter, and damaged a Pakistani naval tanker and shore installations.

Before the Styx missile homing system can acquire the target, Osa-class boats must maintain a straight heading for five minutes before launching the missile. Since in moderate to rough seas they would find it difficult if not impossible to follow a straight course for such a period, launching can only take place in smooth to moderate sea conditions or from a sheltered location.

As a Styx missile approaches its target, its terminal homing seeker takes over. Providing the target is equipped with an electronic countermeasure system to detect the approaching missile, steps can be taken to jam it. In the 'Yom Kippur' war of 1973, the Israelis claim to have successfully employed 'Chaff' – clouds of small aluminium strips dispersed by grenades in the path of the oncoming Styx to provide decoy targets. The concept is similar to that of Window, employed by Allied bombers to baffle German radar operators in World War II.

Chaff grenades are generally tried in groups. In the case of small fast patrol craft, nine will provide a chaff cloud of sufficient echoing area and intensity to protect a craft of 200 tons displacement. The idea is that the missile's radar seeker locks on to and tracks the chaff cloud (in the case of missiles known to employ infra-red seekers, flares are used to provide a decoy) instead of the vessel.

The Osa was the first Soviet fast patrol boat with a steel hull. Like the similar but smaller Komar, its lines are dominated by four large hooded Styx missile launchers mounted in this case in two pairs abreast of the deckhouse. Two variants are in service – Osa I, with slab-sided launchers and the more recent Osa II with cylindrical, elongated dustbin-shaped launchers. Sixty-five Osa Is are in service with the Soviet Navy and fifty-five Osa IIs. In fact the Osa is the world's most widely used missilecraft. Apart from 120 delivered to the Soviet Navy by mid-1978, a further 160 have been transferred to other navies as follows. Algeria 3, Bulgaria 3, China 60, Cuba 5, Egypt 6, Finland 9, East Germany 12, India 8, Iraq 10, North Korea 8, Poland 12, Romania 5, Somalia 3, Syria 6, Yugoslavia 10.

Power Plant: Three 5,000 hp ChNSP Type 56 16/17 diesels, each driving its own propeller shaft.
Hull: Steel.
Crew: 25.
Armament: Four SS-N-2A or 2B Styx missiles. Two twin 30 mm. remote AA mountings, one forward, one aft.
Dimensions: Length overall 39.2 m. (128.7 ft): beam 7.7 m. (25.1 ft): draught 1.8 m. (5.9 ft).
Weights: Displacement, fully loaded 200 tons; standard, 165 tons.
Performance: Maximum operating speed, 32 knots.
Range: 800 n. miles at 25 knots.

27 **P6**, Egypt.
Known originally as the Soviet Type 184, P6 dates back to the early 1950s. It was designed to replace the timber-hulled Edco, Higgins and Vosper patrol torpedo-boats supplied by the United Kingdom and U.S.A. during World War II and like its forebears, has a hard chine hull.

Initially power was supplied by four 900 bhp M-50 diesels which provided a speed of 43 knots. Later versions, the P8, which was equipped with a bow only hydrofoil system and the P10 – both redesigned for anti-submarine warfare – had a gas-turbine installed for improved 'sprint' performance. Air for the gas-turbine was taken in through a midship funnel. Although the P8 has since been retired from service, the bow foil arrangement proved so successful that it was emulated later in the Chinese People's Republic by Shanghai Shipyard on the Hu Chwan (White Swan) class, while in 1973 it was re-introduced in the Soviet Union on the 230-ton Turya diesel-powered FAC, designed for ASW warfare. A number of P6s have been converted for use as radio-controlled targets.

It is thought that nearly 300 of this class were built before production was terminated in 1960. Countries supplied with P6s by the Soviet Union include Algeria 12, China 80, Cuba 12, Egypt 24, East Germany 18, Guinea 4, Indonesia 14, Iraq 12, Nigeria 3, Poland 20, North Vietnam 6, Somalia 4, Tanzania 3 (ex. East German craft).

Power Plant: Standard P6. Thought to be four M-50, M-400 or M-401 diesels. Maximum output (M-400 and M-401) about 1,200 bhp.
Hull: Wooden construction.
Crew: 20 officers and ratings.
Armament: Torpedoes: Two 21 in. Guns: Four 25 mm. cannon in two twin mounts. Facilities for carrying mines or depth charges. Egyptian Navy version has been rearmed with an eight-barrelled 122 mm. rocket launcher forward and a twin 14.5 mm. gun aft.
Dimensions: Length 25.7 m. (84.2 ft): beam 6.1 m. (20.01 ft): draught 1.8 m. (5.91 ft).
Displacement: Standard, 66 tons, fully loaded 75 tons.
Performance: Maximum speed, 43 knots.

28 **PB Mk I and Mk III**, U.S.A.

This new all-aluminium inshore patrol craft is replacing vessels of the Swift type, originally employed by the U.S.

Navy's Coastal Surveillance Force in Vietnam, and which later provided the base design for the Israeli Navy's Dabur.

Two variants are in service: Mk I, with the bridge and deckhouse superstructure sited on the longitudinal centreline and Mk III with the bridge superstructure located on the starboard side in order to provide space for the mounting of grenade launchers, missiles and other weapons on the port side. Only two units of the PB Mk I are in service, both of which have been transferred to the U.S. Naval Reserve Force. Mk II exists as a design only; Mk III is currently in production. Fifteen units are on order for the U.S. Navy and thirteen for the Philippine Navy. The former are being built by Peterson Builders, Sturgeon Bay, Wisconsin, the latter by Sewart Seacraft, Berwick, Louisiana.

Power Plant: Three 530 bhp General Motors Detroit diesels, each driving its own propeller shaft.
Hull: All-welded aluminium construction.
Armament: Mk III: twin mounting at aft end of pilot house and four single manual mounts at each quarter on the main deck. Either 20 mm. cannon or 50 cal. machine-guns at each mount.

Specification for Mk III
Dimensions: Length overall 19.8 m. (65 ft): beam 5.5 m. (18 ft): draught 1.8 m. (5.9 ft).
Displacement: Fully loaded 41 tons, light 31.5 tons.
Performance: Maximum speed about 26 knots.

29 **Paek Ku (Seagull)**, South Korea.
Derived from the U.S. Navy's Asheville class, the Paek Ku missile-launching fast attack craft is one of the highly successful PSMM (Patrol Ship, Multi-Mission) series designed by Tacoma Boatbuilding Co., Tacoma, Washington. The prototype for the Paek Ku series was the ex-U.S. Navy PG96

Benicia, transferred to South Korea in 1971, and operating as PGM 101. Variants have been adopted by the navies of South Korea (eight), Taiwan (fifteen), Saudi Arabia (six) and Indonesia (four, plus an option on another fourteen).

South Korean and the Indonesian PSMMs are powered by six Avco Lycoming gas-turbines driving two propeller shafts, whereas the Taiwan Navy has selected a CODAG (Combined Diesel and Gas Turbine) propulsion system employing three 5,000 shp Avco Lycoming gas-turbines and three 960 hp diesels driving three propeller shafts. The six Saudi Arabian craft employ a different CODAG system comprising a single 16,500 shp General Electric LM1500 gas-turbine and two 1,500 hp Cummins diesels driving two shafts.

Pennant Nos/Class Names/Year of Commissioning
  Republic of Korea: 102 Paek Ku 12, 1975: 103 Paek Ku 13, 1975: 105 Paek Ku 15, 1976: 106 Paek Ku 16, 1976: 107 Paek Ku 17, 1977: 108 Paek Ku 18, 1977: 109 Paek Ku 19, 1977. First of this class were built in the United States, the remainder in South Korea.
  Taiwan Navy: Lead craft, under construction in Tacoma during 1977. The remaining fourteen units will be built in Taiwan. Pennant numbers and names not available at the time of going to press.
  Indonesian Navy: All four PSMM Mk 5 craft ordered by the Indonesian Navy are under construction in South Korea by Korea-Tacoma Boatbuilding Co.
  Saudi Arabia: Training of Saudi Arabian personnel to operate the six PSMMs ordered for the Saudi Navy is being undertaken in the United States, where the craft will be built.

Power Plant: Korean PSMMs: Six 2,700 hp Avco Lycoming TF35 gas-turbines driving two shafts, each fitted with a controllable-pitch propeller. Gas-turbines can be introduced singly, in pairs or collectively to provide a range of power

settings. CODAG systems installed in Saudi Arabian and Taiwan craft as described above.
Hull: All-aluminium structure. Superstructure of mixed aluminium glass-fibre construction.
Crew: Five officers, 27 enlisted personnel.
Armament: PSMM Mk 5 Korean Navy: Missiles: Four launchers for standard missiles with 1 reload each. Guns: One Mk 34 76/50 mm. gun forward, one 40 mm. gun aft. Two .50 machine-guns.

Taiwan Navy: Missiles: Four container/launchers for Otomat Mk 2 anti-ship missiles. Guns: Two 30 mm. Emerlec twin mountings. Two 0.50 in. machine-guns.

Saudi Arabia: Missiles: Two twin Harpoon launchers. Guns: One 76 mm. Oto Melara, one 81 mm. mortar, two 40 mm. mortars, two 20 mm. cannon.

Electronics: (Taiwan model): Selenia/SMA RAN-11LX detection radar; Divisione Sistemi Navali Na 10 Med O Fire control: IPNIO data processing and display system.
Dimensions: Length overall 50.2 m. (165 ft): beam 7.3 m. (24 ft): draught 2.3 m. (9.5 ft).
Displacement: Standard 240 tonnes, fully loaded, 270 tonnes.
Performance: Maximum speed, six gas-turbines, 40 knots plus. Maximum speed, Taiwan Navy CODAG models, 40 knots plus/gas-turbines plus diesels. Range (Taiwan model): 2,700 miles at 12 knots with one diesel operating, 1,900 miles at 20 knots with three diesels. Diesels plus gas-turbines at 40 knots plus, 700 miles.

30 **PCHELA (Bee)**, Soviet Union.

Derived from the Strela (Arrow) 82-92 seat hydrofoil passenger ferry, the Pchela is in service with the KGB for frontier patrol duties in the Baltic, Black Sea, Caspian and various other sea areas. Twenty-five are thought to have been built between 1965–1972. Pchela has a fixed, trapeze-type surface-piercing bow foil with a horizontal centre-section between the main struts.

Power Plant: Propulsion machinery is probably the same as that installed on the Strela – two 970 hp 12-cylinder M-50F3 or two 1,000 hp M-401A water-cooled, supercharged, 12-cylinder V-type diesels.
Hull: Welded all-aluminium hull and superstructure.
Armament: Two remotely operated twin machine-gun mounts, one forward, one aft, and depth charges.
Electronics: Pot Drum surveillance radar. High Pole IFF.
Dimensions: Length overall 29.3 m. (96 ft 1 in.): beam 8.3 m. 26 ft 4 in.): draught afloat 2.25 m. (7 ft 7 in.).
Weights: Displacement, full load, about 60 tons.
Performance: Cruising speed 34 knots: max. cruising speed 40 knots, max. sea state capability foilborne 1.22 m. (4 ft) waves.
Foilborne Range: 740 km. approx.

31 **Perkasa**, Malaysia.

Four of these triple-screw, gas-turbine powered fast attack craft were built by Vosper Ltd for the Malaysian Navy during 1964–6. Like the Libyan Susa and the Danish Søløven class, the Perkasa combines a Brave class hull with the form of construction employed on Vosper's demonstration craft, Ferocity. The main hull and deck structure is in glued laminated wood while the bridge and air intakes are in aluminium alloy.

Armed originally with four 21 in. torpedoes, the Perkasa class was converted in 1971 to carry eight SS-12 wire-guided, surface-to-surface missiles.

Pennant Numbers/Class Names/Year of Commissioning
P152 Gempita, 1967: P151 Handalan, 1967: P153 Pendekar, 1967: P150 Perkasa, 1967.
Power Plant: Three Rolls-Royce Proteus gas-turbines, each rated at 3,620 bhp max. and 2,960 continuous, on three

separate shafts, combined with two 230 hp GM diesels on wing shafts for cruising and manoeuvring. Total fuel capacity 25 tons.

Hull: Main hull and deck structure in glued laminated wood. Superstructure, aluminium alloy.

Crew: CO, two officers, three POs and sixteen ratings. Fully air-conditioned work and rest areas.

Armament: Missiles: 8 Aérospatiale SS-12M close-range, surface-to-surface, wire-guided missiles. Eight spare missiles in deck stowage. Max. range 19,650 ft (6000 m.); impact speed 182 knots. Sighting turret and fire control system developed jointly by Aérospatiale and Vosper Thornycroft. Guns: One 40 mm. and one 20 mm. cannon.

Dimensions: Length overall 30.38 m. (99 ft 8 in.), beam 7.78 m. (25 ft 9 in.), draught aft, 2.28 m. (7.3 ft).

Displacement: Standard 95 tons, fully loaded 114 tons.

Performance: Max. speed, 54 knots plus. Max. continuous cruising, 49 knots. Cruising speed on diesels alone, 9 knots.

Range: Gas-turbines only, 644 km. (400 miles); diesels only, 3,220 km. (2,000 miles). Long range deck tanks add further 60.93 km. (100 miles) to range when operating on gas-turbines.

32 **PHM**, United States.

While most NATO Navies contended that hydrofoils of the size of the Boeing Tucumcari, which the U.S. Navy demonstrated in Europe in 1971, was too small for their particular needs, many displayed a strong interest in a very much larger craft employing the same formula – a canard submerged foil configuration and waterjet propulsion. When the U.S. Navy proposed building such a craft, a 230-ton missile-armed fast patrol boat to combat the threat posed in the Mediterranean by craft of the Osa and Komar types, Italy and the Federal Republic of Germany decided to become partners with the U.S. Navy in a project to develop the craft, which became known in Europe as the NATO PHM (Patrol Hydrofoil Missile) Programme. Although orders from Italy and West Germany have not been placed so far, the U.S. Navy ordered a prototype, the PHM-1 USS Pegasus, which was commissioned into service on 9 July 1977, and five follow-on craft, which will be delivered between January 1981 and February 1982. Re-classified Patrol Combatant Missile (Hydrofoils), in June 1975, they will be assigned to a PCM(H) squadron operating in the Mediterranean and will specialize in anti-submarine warfare in coastal waters. Four of the production craft will be armed with a 76 mm. Oto Melara dual-purpose rapid-fire cannon and eight Harpoon anti-ship missiles in two quadruple lightweight canister launchers. The fifth, PHM-6 is expected to be used as a hydrofoil high-speed test craft and will be unarmed.

Foils: Fully submerged canard arrangement. Automatically controlled flaps are fitted to the foil trailing edges to provide control and lift augmentation at take-off and during flight. The one-piece aft foil of shallow 'M' configuration retracts rearwards and the inverted 'T' shaped bow foil retracts forward into a bow recess. The bow foil rotates to provide directional control when foilborne.
Power Plant: Foilborne: Single 18,000 shp, two-stage, two-speed Aerojet waterjet, driven through two sets of reduction gears by a single General Electric LM 2500 marine gas-turbine. Hullborne: Twin Aerojet waterjet pumps powered by two 800 hp MTU 8V33 ITC80 diesels. Steering control in hullborne mode provided by stern rudders which rotate electrohydraulically in response to the wheel.
Hull: Hull and superstructure in all-welded marine aluminium.
Crew: On average 21 officers and ratings, but dependent on weapons carried.
Weapons: Missiles; main armament of the standard U.S. Navy version will be eight McDonnell Douglas AGM-84A

Harpoon anti-ship missiles in two quadruple container-launchers, but Exocet, Otomat, Penguin, Standard or any smaller missile system can be fitted. Guns: Standard primary gun is the 76 mm. Oto Melara cannon, which is automatically controlled by the fire control system. Two Mk 20 Rh 202 20 mm. AA cannon can be provided, one each, on port and starboard wings, immediately aft of bridge.

Dimensions: Length overall, foil struts extended for foilborne operation 40.0 m. (131.2 ft): Maximum width across foils, 14.5 m. (47.5 ft): draught foilborne 2.7 m. (8.9 ft): draught hullborne, foils retracted 2.9 m. (9.4 ft).

Displacement: Fully loaded, 235 tonnes.

Performance: Max. speed in excess of 50 knots. Can negotiate 8–13 ft seas at speeds in excess of 40 knots. Foilborne range in excess of 600 n. miles, hullborne range, in excess of 1,800 n. miles.

33 **Plejad**, Sweden.

Lürssen Werft's first post-World War II order for small warships was placed by the Royal Swedish Navy in 1954. The contract was for eleven 45 m. motor torpedo-boats which became known as the Plejad class. Drawing on their considerable World War II experience with the range of Schnellböte (E-boats) supplies to the German Navy, Lürssen designed and built an outstandingly successful round-bilge craft, powered by three MTU diesels and armed with two 40 mm. Bofors AA guns and six 533 mm. (21 in.) torpedoes.

All eleven units were built at Vegesack between 1954 and 1959. When the Federal German Navy was established in 1955, Lürssen received an order for the design of the Type 140–141, a similar but slightly larger and more powerful craft fitted with four MTU diesels. Lürssen subsequently built twenty-two of this type which entered service between 1958 and 1964 as the Jaguar class.

Of the eleven original members of the Plejad class only

three are currently operational – T107 Aldebaran; T110 Arcturus and T112 Astrea.

Power Plant: Three 3,000 bhp MTU 20V 672 diesels each driving a single fixed-pitch propeller.
Hull: Composite construction, with steel frames, aluminium alloy bulkheads and superstructure and mahogany planking.
Complement: Officers and ratings, 33.
Armament: Torpedoes: Six 533 mm. (21 in.) tubes. Guns: Two single 40 mm. Bofors AA mounts, four 103 mm. and one 12-rail 57 mm. flare rocket launchers.
Dimensions: Length overall 45 m. (147.6 ft), beam 5.9 m. (19.4 ft), draught 1.4 m. (4.6 ft).
Displacement: Fully loaded, 170 tons, standard 155 tons.
Performance: Maximum speed 37.5 knots.

34 **Rade Končar**, Yugoslavia.
Yugoslavia's current naval shipbuilding programme includes ten missile boats of this class which is generally known as the 'Type 211'. The first two units, Rade Končar and Vlado Četkovič, have been completed and a further four are under construction, all at the Titovom Brodogradlistu Yard at Kraljevice. Although the hull of the 'Type 211' appears to have been inspired by that of the Swedish Spica class, it also incorporates a number of the characteristics of the Soviet Shershen and Osa classes, including a rounded deck. Both classes are operated by the Yugoslavian Navy (fourteen Shershens and ten Osas) and several Shershen torpedo-boats were built in Yugoslavia.

Unique in the sense that it is the first missile boat to be built in that country, the Type 211 is also noteworthy for the unusually extensive mixture of European and Soviet technology employed in its outfitting. Its main engines, two Marine Proteus gas-turbines, were purchased from the

United Kingdom, its MTU cruising engines come from the German Federal Republic, its guns and associated electronics were delivered by Swedish companies and the Soviet Union delivered the primary armament – two SS-N-2Bs of the type employed on the Osa II and an increasing number of Soviet destroyers.

Class Names/Launch Dates
Rade Končar, 15.10.76: Vlado Četkovič, 20.8.77:
Power Plant: CODAG system employing two 4,500 bhp Rolls-Royce Marine Proteus gas-turbines for 'sprint' performance and two 3,600 bhp MTU diesels for cruising.
Hull: Welded steel construction. Superstructure and interior bulkheads in light alloy. Round bilge form.
Complement: Officers and ratings, 40.
Armament: Missiles: Two Soviet SS-N-2Bs in launch containers as employed on the Osa II class. Launchers mounted at stern on projecting platforms, angled outwards from longitudinal centreline to permit forward firing. Range 25 n. miles. Infra-red terminal guidance. Guns: Two Swedish Bofors 57 mm. single automatic AA guns, one forward, one aft. Each fires 200 rounds per minute and is capable of being employed against surface targets as well as aircraft and missiles.
Electronics: Main radar, weapon guidance radar and navigational radar supplied by Philips Teleindustrier AB, Fack, Sweden. Soviet made Square Head IFF antenna.
Dimensions: Length overall 45 m. (147.64 ft), beam 8.3 m. (27.23 ft): draught 1.8 m. (5.91 ft).
Displacement: Standard, 240–250 tons.
Performance (approx.): Maximum speed, 40 knots. Range at cruising speed of 35 knots, 500 n. miles.

35 **Reshef (Flash)**, Israel.
Reshef, like its immediate predecessor, the Saar, was designed with the assistance of Lürssen Werft, and bears a

strong similarity to the Federal German Navy's Type 143s. Built at the state-owned Israeli Shipyards Ltd, Haifa, the 415-ton Reshef is 13 m. longer than the Saar and combines a maximum continuous cruising speed of 25–30 knots with the range of a destroyer. Main armament generally comprises two 76 mm. Oto Melara dual-purpose cannon and either six or seven Gabriel missiles. For close-in air defence, a 20 mm. Oerlikon cannon and a 12.7 mm. machine-gun are mounted aft of the bridge. Port and starboard torpedo tubes and depth charges can also be fitted if required.

Although intended chiefly for operation in the Red Sea several Reshefs are operating in the Mediterranean to protect Israel's sea-lanes and her western coastline.

The first six Reshef class vessels were built between February 1973 and January 1975. The first two members of the class, the Reshef and the Keshet, were ready in time to play major roles in the Yom Kippur war in October 1973. Exercises with ten Saars and the two Reshef boats took place off Crete on the night of 4–5 October 1973, and on Saturday 7 October, off the Syrian port of Latakia came the world's first action between fast missilecraft. Reports leave no doubt that the tactics employed by the commanders of the Reshef and Saar class boats proved vastly superior. In fact the Syrians lost both their original Osas and three Komars. Two nights later a second action took place off the Egyptian coast during which the Egyptian navy lost four Osas and two Komars.

Normal zones of operation for Israel's Reshefs and Saars are the narrow shipping lanes extending from the home coastline to the eastern shores of Sicily (an area which encompasses Crete but which lies to the south of Cyprus) and from Sharm-el-Sheik, at the mouth of the Gulf of Aqaba, to the mouth of the Red Sea in the Straits of Bab-al-Mandab. Patrols in the Mediterranean are aimed at protecting Israeli shipping lanes while those in the Red Sea are regarded as being of tactical importance.

Close support is provided by the Israeli air force, which

flies McDonnell Douglas F-4 Phantoms for naval reconnaissance and gives combat assistance in response to instructions from Israeli navy commanders at sea.

Two developments scheduled to improve the combat effectiveness of the Reshef are the option of the U.S. Navy's Harpoon missile, which has a range of about 50 miles, and the acquisition of a surveillance of 'spotter' helicopter like the Israeli Aircraft Industry's Westwind to provide the missile craft with earlier detection capability. At present targets can be picked up on the Reshef surveillance radar at a range of up to only 14 n. miles. Westwinds, presumably would provide external mid-course guidance to enable the Harpoons and the longer-range Gabriel IIs to hit more distant targets.

Illustrations of the range, seaworthiness and reliability of this class were the appearance of two Reshefs in July 1976 in New York and the deployment of four to Eilat, on the Red Sea, necessitating a voyage of some 14,000 km. (8,699 miles) via the Straits of Gibraltar and the Cape of Good Hope. It is reported that the vessels were ready for action again the morning after they arrived. This performance so impressed the South African navy that it ordered six for its own use. These are currently under construction in Haifa and Durban. Production is currently being concentrated on the Mk 2 model of the Reshef, the hull of which has been stretched by 3.5 m. to 61.7 m. and the loaded displacement raised to 440 tons.

Reshef I
Hull: Composite transverse framed construction. Frames, bulkheads and deck beams in welded light alloy, longitudinal floor beams and machinery platform in welded steel.
Power Plant: Four MTU diesels, each 2,670 bhp.
Complement/Accommodation: Fully air-conditioned living spaces for crew of 45–48.
Armament: Generally six Gabriel missiles aft, plus two 76 mm. Oto Melara general purpose rapid-firing mounts

for AA defence and surface target engagement, one forward and one aft.
Dimensions: Length overall 58 m. (190.6 ft): beam 7.8 m. (25 ft): draught 2.4 m. (8 ft).
Displacement: Fully loaded, 415 tons.
Performance: Maximum speed 30–32 knots, maximum continuous speed 25–30 knots, cruising speed 20 knots.
Reshef II
Crew: 48.
Armament: As for Reshef I but with two twin 30 mm. rapid-fire mounts either side of the bridge deck for close-in AA defence. Surface to air missiles can be fitted, also torpedo tubes and depth charges to replace aft 76 mm. mount.
Dimensions: Length overall 61.7 m.
Displacement: Fully loaded, 440 tons.
Performance: Maximum speed 32 knots. High-powered variant on offer, fitted with four 4,000 bhp MTU 16 cylinder V-type diesels and capable of 36 knots.

36 **Saar I, II and III**, Israel.

Arguably the most battle-tested of today's missile boats, the Saar class was initiated in 1965 after Israeli defence planners had been alerted to the danger of the growing numbers of Russian-built Komars and Osas being operated by the Arab navies. In the absence of an indigenous yard suitable for warship production at that time an approach was made to one of the world's foremost small warship builders, Lürssen Werft of Bremen-Vegesack, to design and build six 45 m. (147.6 ft) fast patrol craft for delivery in 1968. Although originally the craft were to be fitted with torpedo-tubes and 40 mm. AA guns, it was the intention of the Israeli navy to refit the craft on arrival with their own sea-skimming missile, the Gabriel.

News of the Israeli intention reached the ears of the West German government, which immediately banned the placing of the order for fear of upsetting West German–Arab relations. Lürssen, however, was permitted to pass on the drawings to a French yard – Constructions Mécaniques de Normandie, at Cherbourg, which subsequently built two batches of six craft.

The first batch was ordered in 1966, each craft being fitted with three 40 mm. AA guns and sonar. Craft of the second group were each fitted with a 76 mm. Oto Melara dual-purpose gun forward. In late 1969, the French government placed an embargo on any further sales of arms to Israel, after only seven of the twelve craft had been delivered. The Israelis however, decided to evade the embargo and the crews of the remaining five craft set out from Cherbourg on Christmas Eve 1969, and successfully whisked them away to Haifa, where they arrived in excellent condition a few weeks later. This incident received world-wide publicity.

During the Yom Kippur war large numbers of Syrian and Egyptian vessels and Mediterranean port facilities were attacked by Saars with relative impunity. One of the handicaps faced by the Israeli missile craft during the October War of 1973, was the considerable difference in range between the Styx missiles employed by the Arab States involved and that of Israel's Gabriel Mk 1. Unconfirmed, but generally reliable sources put the range of the former at 20 n. miles and the latter at 14 n. miles, resulting in a danger gap of 6 n. miles. However, Israeli commanders successfully employed a combination of EW countermeasures, high-speed manoeuvring and their rapid-firing 76 mm. Oto Melara automatic cannon to combat the Styx, at least ten of which were knocked down. The Saar class is expected to have a service life of about ten years. Eventually it will be replaced by the Flagstaff II hydrofoil missilecraft.

Power Plant: Four 3,300 hp MTU diesels, each coupled through reversible gearboxes to four shafts fitted with three-bladed fixed-pitch propellers.

Hull: All-welded, prefabricated steel. Aluminium superstructure.
Complement/Accommodation: Crew 35–40. All living and operating spaces air-conditioned.
Armament: Latest available reports state that the twelve craft have been divided into three variants with weapon fits as follows: Saar I, two 40 mm. AA guns and five Gabriels; Saar II, one 40 mm. mount and eight Gabriels; Saar III, one Oto Melara 76 mm. dual-purpose rapid-fire gun and six Gabriels. Four torpedo tubes can be fitted to the latter if required.
Dimensions: Length overall 45 m. (147.6 ft): beam 7 m. (23 ft): draught 2.5 m. (8.2 ft).
Displacement: Standard 220 tons; fully loaded 250 tons.
Performance: Maximum speed, about 40 knots.
Range: 2,500 n. miles at 15 knots, 1,600 n. miles at 20 knots and 1,000 n. miles at 30 knots.

37 **Sarancha**, Soviet Union.
Operational evaluation trials of the Sarancha began in the Eastern Baltic in mid-1977. Thought to be the forerunner of a new class of extremely formidable missilecraft, the vessel is armed with four SS-N-9 anti-ship missiles, a retractable rapid-firing ship-to-air missile system and a fully automatic twin 30 mm. AA cannon. The foil system is of combined surface-piercing and submerged configuration reminiscent of that employed in the United States on the experimental Grumman Denison. A sonic/electronic automatic control system (ACS) adjusts lift by operating trailing edge flaps on each foil. The system ensures that vertical and lateral accelerations are kept within specified limits to prevent excessive loads on the structure and also that the vessel provides a stable platform from which anti-ship missiles can be launched accurately while travelling at speed in rough seas.

The chief advantage of employing surface piercing bow foils is that they will provide inherent stability in the event of the ACS system failing, enabling the craft to return to its base foilborne in all but the most severe sea conditions. In the event of a complete ACS failure in a fully submerged craft, it would have to return hullborne at a greatly reduced speed and with a substantial increase in fuel consumption.

All three foil/strut units retract upwards completely clear of the water for docking and shipping.

Power Plant: Two marinized gas-turbines. Power is transmitted to the two propellers at the base of each strut through two sets of bevel gears and two vertical shafts.

Armament: Four SS-N-9 ship-to-ship missiles mounted in four lightweight launchers, one pair each side of the deckhouse forward; one SA-N-4 surface-to-air missile launcher on forward deck and one twin 23 mm. rapid fire AA cannon aft.

Radar and Fire Control: Band Stand radar to activate SS-N-9s; Fish Bowl radar to operate SA-N-4 launcher and Bass Tilt fire control for the twin 23 mm. fully automatic close-in AA cannon, High Pole, IFF and Square Head radar/IFF interrogator.

Dimensions: Length overall, 45 m. (147 ft 8 in.): width, foils extended 23 m. (75 ft): hull beam, 10 m. (32 ft 10 in.): draught hullborne, foils retracted, 2 m. (6 ft 7 in.).

Displacement: Normal take-off displacement, 330 tonnes.

Performance: Maximum speed, foilborne 50-52 knots.

38 **Scimitar**, United Kingdom.

Scimitar and its two sister craft, Cutlass and Sabre, are employed by the Royal Navy to instruct the crews of larger warships in the techniques of countering attacks by fast missilecraft. Developed from the earlier Brave class, the Scimitar employs a similar hard-chine planing hull of glued laminated wood, but instead of the triple Proteus gas-turbines of the former, it has a twin Proteus arrangement, although provision is made for the installation of a third unit if required.

In training exercises, the role of these fast training craft is to simulate attacks on NATO naval forces by Soviet Osas and Komars. Normally these craft operate unarmed but a forward gun can be fitted should the craft be needed for operational purposes.

Pennant Nos/Class Names/Commissioning Dates
P274 Cutlass (12.11.70): P275 Sabre (5.3.71): P271 Scimitar (19.7.70):
Power Plant: CODAG system, comprising two Rolls-Royce gas-turbines and two Foden diesels for cruising. Provision for installation of third Proteus.
Hull: Glued laminated wood.
Crew: Two officers and ten ratings.
Armament: None carried. 40 mm. mount can be provided.
Dimensions: Length overall 30.5 m. (100 ft): beam 8.1 m. (26 ft 6 in.): draught 1.9 m. (6.4 ft).
Displacement: Fully loaded, 102 tons.
Performance: Max. speed, 40 knots. Range, 425 n. miles at 35 knots; 1,500 n. miles at 11.5 knots.

39 **Sea Wolf**, Singapore.

In order to broaden its international base, Lürssen has established several subsidiary companies abroad and licensed a number of overseas shipyards to construct Lürssen-designed vessels. During 1969, in south-east Asia, the company founded the Hong Leong-Lürssen Shipyard Ltd, at Kuala Lumpur, with a yard located at Butterworth, and also came to a licensing agreement with Singapore Shipbuilding & Engineering Ltd (Singapore). Since then, in addition to ship repair work, the Butterworth Yard has built nine river landing craft, four missilecraft for Thailand, two for Singapore and a research vessel for Malaysia.

The first two 48 m. TNC 48 Sea Wolf class missilecraft were built at Vegesack, arriving in Singapore in the autumn of 1972, but the remaining four were built locally between 1972–1975 by the Singapore Shipbuilding & Engineering Co. A feature of the armament is the employment of IAI Gabriel missiles.

Power Plant: Four 3,800 hp MTU lightweight marine diesels, each driving its own fixed-pitch propeller.
Crew: Forty officers and ratings.
Armament: Five Gabriel ship-to-ship missiles, two Bofors guns, one 57 mm. and one 40 mm.
Fire Control: HSA type M27.
Dimensions: Length overall 48 m. (158 ft): max. beam 7 m. (23 ft): draught 2.3 m. (7 ft 6 in.).
Weight: Displacement, fully loaded, 230 tons.
Performance: Cruising speed, 34 knots.

40 **Shanghai I–IV**, Chinese People's Republic.
Series production of the 'Shanghai' class of fast gunboat has been in progress at the Shanghai Naval Shipyard and several other Chinese yards since the early 1960s. More than 350 craft of this class had been completed by mid-1977, some 65 of which had been transferred to the navies of other countries including North Korea, Pakistan, Romania, Tanzania and Sierra Leone.

Several variants are in service, each differing mainly in bridge outline, the number and calibre of guns fitted and the positions in which they are installed. Intended, apparently, to meet a variety of operational contingencies, each variant can be fitted with mine rails, torpedo tubes and depth charges.

Power Plant: Four 1,200 bhp M-50, M-401 or similar marine diesels each driving its own propeller shaft.
Crew: Twenty-five officers and ratings.

Armament: 'Type I', one 57 mm. gun forward, twin 37 mm. gun aft. 'Type II', one 57 mm. gun forward, one twin 25 mm. mount aft of deckhouse, and one twin 37 mm. gun aft. 'Types III–IV', one twin 37 mm. gun forward, one twin 25 mm. mount aft of bridge deckhouse, and one twin 37 mm. mount aft. Sightings have been made of vessels of this class mounting a twin 75 mm. recoilless rifle forward.
Dimensions: Length overall 39 m. (128 ft): beam 5.5 m. (18 ft): draught 1.7 m. (5.6 ft).
Displacement: Standard 120 tons, fully loaded about 155 tons.
Performance: Maximum speed about 30 knots.

41 **Shershen**, Soviet Union.
Production of this diesel-powered class of fast attack torpedo-boats began in 1963. In addition to the fifty Shershens delivered to the Soviet Navy, four have been delivered to the Bulgarian Navy, fifteen to East Germany, six to Egypt, thirteen to Yugoslavia and four to North Korea.

Power Plant: Three 3,250 hp marine diesels, each driving its own propeller shaft.
Crew: 16.
Armament: Four (21 in.) torpedo tubes, twelve depth charges, two twin 30 mm. automatic cannon mounts.
Dimensions: Length overall 35.2 m. (115.5 ft): beam 7 m. (23.1 ft): draught 1.6 m. (5 ft).
Weights: Maximum loaded displacement, 160 tons, standard base weight 150 tons.
Performance: Max. speed, calm water 40 knots.
Electronics: Surveillance radar, Pot Drum; fire control, Drum Tilt; IFF, High Pole, IFF interrogator, Square Head.

42 **Snögg**, Norway.
Based on the 36.5 m. hull of the earlier Storm class, Snögg has been built by Bätservis Werft A/S, of Mandal, Norway – the

company responsible for the highly successful Nasty class fast attack craft. A feature of the Snögg is its combination of two forms of armament, Penguin anti-ship missiles and 21 in. torpedoes.

Class Names/Year of Commissioning:
P985 Kjapp, 1971; P984 Kvikk, 1971; P981 Rapp, 1970; P983 Rask, 1971; P982 Snar, 1970; P980 Snögg, 1970.
Power Plant: Two 3,600 bhp MTU supercharged diesels, each driving its own propeller shaft.
Hull: Steel.
Complement: 18.
Armament: Four Kongsberg Vaapenfabrik Penguin anti-ship missiles, four 21 in. torpedoes and one 40 mm. dual-purpose gun forward.
Dimensions: Length overall 36.5 m. (120 ft); beam 6.2 m. (20.5 ft); draught 1.5 m. (4.9 ft).
Fire Control System: Kongsberg SM-3.
Displacement: Standard 100 tons, fully loaded 125 tons.
Performance: Maximum speed about 32 knots.

43 **Søløven**, Denmark.
Similar in power arrangements and construction to Libya's Susa class, the Søløven is based on the hull of the Brave Borderer and Brave Swordsmen, operated by the Trials and Special Service Squadron of the British Royal Navy during the 1960s. Power is supplied by three Rolls-Royce Proteus marine gas-turbines for sprint performance and by two GM diesels on wing shafts for cruising. The first two craft of this series were built by Vosper Ltd, and the remaining three by the Royal Dockyard, Copenhagen. Unlike the Susa class, which has been rearmed with missiles, the Søløven retains its main armament of four 21 in. torpedoes.

Pennant Nos/Class Names/Date of Commissioning:
P510 Søløven, 12.2.65: P511 Søridderen, 10.2.65: P512

Søbjornen, 9.65: P513 Søhesten, 6.66: P514 Søhunden, 12.66: P515 Søulven 3.67.

Power Plant: Three Rolls-Royce Proteus gas-turbines, each rated at 3,620 bhp max. and 2,960 bhp continuous on three separate shafts, combined with two 230 hp GM diesels on wing shafts for cruising and manoeuvring.

Hull: Main hull and deck structure, wood. Superstructure, aluminium alloy.

Crew: 29.

Armament: Torpedoes, four 21 in. in side launchers. Guns, two 40 mm. Bofors, one forward, one aft.

Dimensions: Length overall 30.38 m. (99 ft 8 in.); beam 7.78 m. (25 ft 9 in.); draught aft 2.28 m. (7.3 ft).

Displacement: Standard, 95 tons, fully loaded, 114 tons.

Performance: Maximum speed 54 knots, max. continuous cruising, 49 knots. Cruising speed on diesels alone 9–10 knots.

Range: Gas-turbines only, 644 km. (400 miles), diesels only 3,220 km. (2,000 miles).

44 **Sparviero**, Italy.

Derived from the U.S. Navy's PGH-2 Tucumcari, the little P420 Sparviero class of hydrofoil missilecraft combines a speed of 50 knots with heavy firepower and the unique all-weather capability of a submerged foil craft. With the exception of the bridge, almost the entire weather deck space is occupied either by weapons or a deckhouse containing their electronic support equipment. Ahead of the deckhouse superstructure is a dual-purpose 76 mm. automatic Oto Melara rapid-firing cannon, while at the aft end are two fixed launchers for Otomat, Sea Killer or Exocet missiles. Electronic equipment includes an Elsag NA-10 gunfire and missile launch control system, surveillance radar, tracking radar, an automatic navigation system with visual displays and an IFF system.

The foils are arranged in canard configuration, with the main foils, which bear about 65 per cent. of the weight, located aft. An electronic/ultrasonic stabilization system controls the craft from the moment of take-off to touchdown, in heave when the craft rises vertically in response to the wave motion, and about all three axes – pitch, roll and yaw. The system incorporates two gyros, one to sense pitch and roll, the other to sense yaw, plus three accelerometers to sense heave. An ultrasonic height sensor detects and maintains a 'flying height' of 1.05 m. (3 ft 5¼ in.) between the keel and the mean water level. Sensor information is transmitted to a solid state computer which calculates the amount of correction necessary to maintain boat stability and/or the pre-selected flying height, and deflects the hydrofoil control flaps accordingly through servo-mechanisms.

To enhance directional stability in shallow water and to prevent the foil tips from suddenly breaking the water surface, while turning at speed in rough water, the aft foils are anhedral. To facilitate maintenance and assist hullborne manoeuvring in shallow waters all three foils are retractable. The aft foils retract sideways and the bow foil retracts forward into a recess in the bow.

The first craft, given the design name Swordfish, was delivered to the Italian navy in July 1974 following a year of operational evaluation trials. An order for a further six was placed by the Italian navy in February 1976.

Power Plant: Foilborne power is supplied by a gas-turbine driven waterjet propulsion system. A single 4,500 shp Rolls-Royce Proteus 15M/553 gas-turbine drives a single double-volute, double-suction twin-impeller centrifugal pump, rated at 106,000 lit./min. (23,315 gall./min.). Water is taken in through forward inlets on each aft foil at the foil/strut intersection and flows up through the hollow interiors of the struts to the pump. From the pump the water is discharged through twin, fixed area nozzles beneath the hull.

In hullborne mode the Sparviero is propelled by a 160 shp General Motors 6V-53 diesel belt-driving a Schottel-Werft steerable propeller outdrive unit mounted on the transom centreline.

Hull: All-welded aluminium hull. Superstructure riveted and welded.

Complement/Accommodation: Typical crew comprises two officers and eight enlisted men. Air-conditioning throughout manned spaces.

Armament: Single 76 mm. Oto Melara rapid-fire dual-purpose cannon, two fixed missile launchers and two anti-ship missiles – Otomat, Seakiller or Exocet.

Navigation, radar and fire control: Selenia SMA model 3RM7-250B performs navigation and search operations with master indicator, rayplot and variable marker. Selenia RTN-10X tracking radar and Elsag NA-10 weapon control system. IFF system comprises IFF/ATC transponder and an IFF interrogator coupled to the radar.

Radio: HF-SSB transceiver and a UHF transceiver.

Dimensions: Length overall, 22.95 m. (75 ft 4 in.): length, foils retracted, 24.6 m. (80 ft 7 in.): width across foils 10.8 m. (35 ft 4 in.): max. beam 7 m. (23 ft).

Displacement: Maximum loaded displacement 64 tonnes.

Performance: Maximum intermittent speed, calm water 50 knots; foilborne continuous speed in sea state 4, 38–40 knots. Hullborne continuous speed, foils down, 7.6 knots. Foilborne range at max. continuous speed of 45 knots, up to 400 n. miles. Hullborne range, up to 1,150 n. miles. Endurance five days.

45/46/47 **Spica I, II and Spica M**, Sweden.

Sweden's gas-turbine powered Spica II fast attack craft is descended from the highly successful Lürssen-designed S-boats operated by the German Navy during World War II. A batch of six Spicas was built during 1965-1966, three by Götaverken, Göteborg and three by Karlskronavarvet AB at Karlskrona, Sweden. In June 1970, the Royal Swedish Navy awarded the latter a second contract for twelve units of an improved version, the Spica II. At the time it was the biggest single order for patrol boats ever placed with the Swedish shipyard. Spicas represent the Royal Swedish Navy's main striking force at sea.

Compared with the earlier model, Spica II has greater length, its displacement has been increased and both its weapons-fit and machinery installations have been up-dated. As with a growing number of modern small fast multi-screw warships and patrol craft, both Spica variants combine gas-turbines with controllable-pitch propulsion. Advantages offered by this arrangement include an appreciable increase in operating flexibility and simplified manoeuvring.

Class Names/Commissioning Dates:

Spica I: T123 Capella 1966; T124 Castor 1967; T122 Sirius 1966; T121 Spica 1966; T125 Vega 1967; T126 Virgo 1967:

Spica II: T140 Halmstad 9 April 1976; T139 Lulea 28 November 1975: T131 Norrköping 11 March 1973; T133 Norrtälje 1 February 1974; T132 Nynäshamn 28 September 1973. T134 Varberg 13 June 1974; T135 Västerås 25 October 1974; T136 Västervik 15 January 1975; T137 Umeä 15 May 1975; T138 Pitea 13 September 1975; T141 Strömstad 13 September 1976; T142 Ystad 10 January 1976.

Power Plant: Spica I. Three Bristol Siddeley Proteus 1274 gas-turbines, each delivering 4,240 shp. Spica II. Three 4,300 shp Rolls-Royce Marine Proteus gas-turbines, each driving, via a Zahnradfabrik MS 710 vee-drive reduction gearbox a 3-bladed KMW controllable-pitch propeller. Craft can be operated on one, two or three engines according to speed required.

Hull: Steel construction. Superstructure and interior bulkheads in light alloy.

Crew: Officers and ratings – thirty approximately.
Armament: Spica I and II: Single Bofors L/70, 57 mm. lightweight multi-purpose gun mounted forward. Magazine holds 40 rounds, sufficient to engage two or three aerial targets. Further 128 rounds carried in racks on traversing platform. Rate of fire, 200 rounds/minute. Chaff rockets on rails on either side of Bofors cupola.
Missiles: Two twin missile launchers expected to be fitted aft on both Spica I and Spica II in place of aft pair of torpedo-tubes in late 1970s.
Torpedoes: Spica II. Battery of six TP61 533 mm. (21 in.) long-range wire-guided torpedoes. This type is also in use by the Danish and Norwegian navies.
Mine Laying: Mine rail fitted.
Dimensions: Length overall, 43.6 m. (144 ft): beam 7.1 m. (23 ft): draught 1.6 m. (5.2 ft).
Displacement: Spica I, Standard, 200, fully loaded, 230 tons. Spica II, Standard, 230.
Performance: Maximum speed, in excess of 35 knots.

Spica M
Based on the 43.6 m. hull of the Spica II, this new model is specially tailored for the export market. Although the torpedo armament of the earlier Spicas is well suited to the tactical needs of the Royal Swedish Navy in the narrows of the Stockholm archipelago, navies faced with defending more open waters require weapons with a substantially greater range. In Spica M, this need has been met by the installation of four Exocet missiles in two twin launchers aft, in the space previously occupied by the Spica II's after torpedo tubes. Since the existing deck space aft of the wheelhouse was insufficient for the two twin Exocet launchers and a Bofors 40 mm. L70 gun at the stern, the complete deckhouse superstructure has been shifted forward to the centre of the craft.

The second major change from the earlier Spicas is the

replacing of the triple Rolls-Royce Proteus gas-turbines by three 3,600 bhp MTU marine diesels. Factors influencing this decision were the need to reduce operating costs and an appreciation of the maintenance problems that gas-turbines would have introduced when the craft was sold to the smaller navies. The first four Spica Ms have been ordered by Malaysia, with building spaced over the period 1977–1979.

Power Plant: Three 3,600 bhp MTU diesels each driving via a vee-drive reduction gearbox a 3-bladed KMW controllable-pitch propeller.
Hull: Steel construction. Six watertight divisions. Superstructure and interior bulkheads in light alloy.
Crew: Officers and ratings, 27.
Armament: Missiles: Four Exocets in two twin launchers. Single Bofors 57 mm. L/70 gun forward in plastic cupola, single Bofors 40 mm. L/70 cannon aft. 67 mm. chaff rockets on rail mounts on either side of the 57 mm. Bofors cupola.
Electronics: Swedish Philips 9LV200 Mk 2 fire control system. Main sensors are an X-band search radar and a Ku-band tracking radar with a bore-sighted TV camera. Laser rangefinder or infra-red tracker optional.
Dimensions: Length overall, 43.6 m.: beam 7.1 m: draught at propellers 3.9 m.
Displacement: Fully loaded 240 tons.
Performance: Max. speed, 37.5 knots: max. continuous speed 34.5 knots.

48 **Stenka**, Soviet Union.
A further derivative of the ubiquitous Osa, the Stenka employs the same basic steel hull, but is designed primarily for offshore anti-submarine patrol. Production began in 1967 at a rate of about five a year and sixty are believed to be in service.

Power Plant: Probably three 5,000 hp Type 56 ChNSP 16/17 diesels, each driving its own propeller shaft.
Hull: Steel.
Crew: 25.
Armament: Four 405 mm. (16 in.) anti-submarine torpedo tubes, depth charges and two twin 30 mm. automatic AA mounts, one forward, one aft.
Dimensions: Length overall 33.9 m. (128.7 ft): beam 7.7 m. (25.1 ft): draught 1.8 m. (5.9 ft).
Weights: Displacement, fully loaded, 210 tons, standard, 170 tons.
Performance: Maximum speed, calm conditions, 33 knots.
Radar: Search and navigation, Pot Drum. Fire control, Drum Tilt. IFF, square.
Sonar: A number of these vessels are equipped with lightweight dipping sonar similar to that carried by the Soviet Navy's Kamov Ka-25, Hormone ASW helicopter.

49 **Storm**, Norway.
Designed in 1961–62 as a new class of gunboat, the Storm series entered production in 1965. During 1970 they underwent conversion into missilecraft following the introduction of Norway's Penguin surface-to-surface missile. Twenty vessels of this type were built by Bergens MV and Westermoen A/S between 1966 and 1968 and all are currently in service.

The Penguin missile has been designed to inflict as much damage as possible on heavily armed adversaries up to the size of a destroyer. It employs inertial guidance for the cruising phase of its flight and passive infra-red homing to guide it to the target for the terminal phase. The missile is fired from a deck-mounted box-launcher and following launch, follows a programmed trajectory towards the predicted impact area. Employment of this system leaves the vessel free to take evasive action immediately after launching a missile or to engage another target. Cruising speed of the Penguin is Mach. 7 and its range is in excess of 11 n. miles.

Class Names/Commissioning Dates:
P968 Arg, 1966: P961 Blink, 1965: P970 Brann, 1967: P977 Brask, 1967: P974 Brott, 1967: P966 Djerv, 1966: P962 Glimt, 1966: P979 Gnist, 1968: P972 Hvass, 1967: P965 Kjekk, 1966: P975 Odd, 1967: P978 Rokk, 1968: P963 Skjold, 1966: P967 Skudd, 1966: P969 Steil, 1967: P960 Storm, 1968: P973 Traust, 1967: P971 Tross, 1967: P964 Trygg, 1966: P976 Pil, 1967.
Power Plant: Two, 3,600 bhp MTU supercharged marine diesels, each driving its own propeller shaft.
Hull: Steel.
Armament: Six Penguin missiles aft. One 3 in. naval mounting forward and one 40 mm. rapid-fire cannon aft.
Fire Control System: Kongsberg Vaapenfabrik SM-3.
Dimensions: Length overall 36.5 m (120 ft): beam 6.2 m. (20.5 ft): draught 1.5 m. (4.9 ft).
Performance: Maximum speed, about 32 knots.

50 **Susa**, Libya.
Susa class FPBs were the first operational naval vessels to be armed with Aérospatiale SS-12M wire-guided, surface-to-surface missiles. Three of these 114-ton boats each powered by three 3,620 bhp Rolls-Royce Proteus gas-turbines and capable of speeds in excess of 54 knots, were ordered from Vosper-Thornycroft in 1966. They became operational with the Libyan navy in 1967–68, armed with eight SS-12M missiles each. The weapons have a destructive power of a 4.5 in. shell. The basic design is similar to that of the Royal Danish Navy's Søløven class, which is in turn a combination of Brave class hull and Ferocity-type construction.

Pennant Numbers/Class Names/Launch Dates:
P01 Susa 31.8.67, P02 Sirte 10.1.68, P03 Sebha 29.2.68.

Power Plant: Three Rolls-Royce Proteus gas-turbines, each rated at 3,620 bhp max. and 2,960 bhp continuous, on three separate shafts, combined with two 230 hp GM diesels on wing shafts for cruising and manoeuvring. Total fuel capacity, 25 tons.

Hull: Main hull and deck structure, wood; superstructure, aluminium alloy.

Complement/Accommodation: Crew comprises CO, two officers, three POs and 16 ratings. Fully air-conditioned work and rest areas.

Armament: Missiles: 8 Aérospatiale SS-12M close-range, surface-to-surface wire-guided missiles, 8 spare missiles in deck stowages. Max. range 6,000 m. (19,650 ft); impact speed 182 knots. Sighting turret and FC system developed jointly by Aérospatiale and Vosper-Thornycroft. Guns: Two 40/60 British Admiralty-type 40 mm. rapid-fire cannon. Torpedoes: Facilities for fitting four torpedoes and side launchers.

Dimensions: Length overall 30.38 m. (99 ft 8 in.): beam max. 7.78 m. (25 ft 9½ in.): draught aft 2.28 m. (7 ft 3 in.).

Displacement: Standard 95 tons, fully loaded 114 tons.

Performance: Max. speed 54 knots plus; max. continuous cruising 49 knots. Cruising speed on diesels alone 9 knots.

Range: Gas-turbines only, 400 miles (644 km.); diesels only 2,000 miles (3,220 km.). Long-range deck tanks add further 160.93 km. (100 miles) to range when operating on gas-turbines.

51 **Tenacity**, United Kingdom.

Tenacity, purchased by the Royal Navy in 1972 for counter missilecraft exercises and fishery protection, was completed by Vosper-Thornycroft in early 1969 as a private venture test and demonstration craft. Its purpose was to establish the merits of a projected 43 m. fast patrol boat design for the 1970s, capable of engaging much larger ships in battle and of defending itself against attack by aircraft and guided missiles. The craft had to have the capability of remaining at sea for up to a week at a time in any reasonable weather and also had to have a high sprint speed.

Various forms of armament were mounted on the craft in mock-up form, ballasting being provided to ensure that the displacement, trim and stability were simulated as closely as possible during exhaustive trials in the open sea.

In Tenacity the main weapon simulated was the Contraves beam-riding Sea-Killer missile with a range of 20 km. and a hitting power comparable to that of a 6 in. shell. The anti-aircraft and anti-missile defence is provided by a twin 35 mm. Oerlikon gun. Both weapons can be controlled simultaneously by the Contraves Seahunter fire-control system, which incorporates a tracking radar and television camera for visual tracking mounted on a combined stabilized platform on the mast. The first result of the Tenacity demonstrations was an order for six Constitución class fast patrol boats for the Venezuelan Navy.

Pennant No./Class Name/Year of Commissioning:
P276 Tenacity, 1973.
Power Plant: Three 4,250 bhp Rolls-Royce Marine Proteus gas-turbines on three separate shafts. Two six-cylinder Paxman Ventura 6-cylinder diesels on wing shafts for cruising and manoeuvring.
Hull: Welded steel main hull. Upper deck and superstructure in partly welded, partly riveted marine aluminium alloys. Beamy, round bilge form with forward knuckle to deflect spray.
Crew: Four officers, 28 ratings.
Dimensions: Length 44.07 m. (144.5 ft); beam 8.09 m. (26.5 ft); draught 2.36 m. (7 ft 9 in.).
Displacement: Standard 165 tons, fully loaded 220 tons.
Performance: Maximum sprint speed 40 knots. Cruising speed (diesels only) 16 knots. Range 2,500 miles at 15 knots.

52 **Tjeld**, Norway.

The 82 ton, 45 knot Tjeld class is derived from the Nasty class built by Båtservis of Mandal, Norway in the early 1960s. Nineteen of these wooden-hulled fast attack torpedo-boats are currently in service with the Norwegian Navy and a variant is in series production in Turkey.

Class Names/Year of Commissioning:
   P343 Tjeld, 1960; P345 Teist, 1960; P348 Stegg, 1961; P380 Skrei, 1962; P344 Skarv, 1960; P382 Sel, 1963; P357 Ravn, 1961; P387 Lyr, 1966; P347 Lom, 1961; P384 Laks, 1964; P385 Knurr, 1966; P346 Jo, 1961; P383 Hval, 1964; P349 Hauk, 1961; P381 Hai, 1962; P388 Gribb, 1962; P389 Geir, 1962; P350 Falk, 1961; P390 Erle, 1966; P386 Delfin, 1966.
Power Plant: Two 18-cylinder Paxman Deltic charge-air cooled, turbocharged diesels, each developing 3,100 bhp and each driving its own propeller shaft.
Hull: Mahogany – fibreglass – mahogany sandwich.
Complement: Three officers, sixteen enlisted men.
Armament: One 40 mm. gun forward, one 20 mm. gun aft, plus four 21 in. (553 mm.) torpedo tubes.
Dimensions: Length 24.5 m. (80.3 ft): beam 7.5 m. (24.5 ft): draught 2.1 m. (6.8 ft).
Displacement: Standard 70 tons; fully loaded 82 tons.
Performance: Maximum speed 45 knots. Range, 450 miles at 40 knots; 1,000 miles at 25 knots.

53 **Turya**, Soviet Union.

Latest of the Eastern bloc military hydrofoils to go into production is the Turya-class torpedo-boat, the first of which made its debut in the Eastern Baltic in the spring of 1972. Based on a standard Osa fast patrol boat hull, it is equipped with a fixed surface-piercing trapeze foil at the bow only. This increases its speed in relatively calm conditions, improves its seakeeping ability and reduces its wave impact response which enhances its performance as a weapons platform. At between 20 and 23 knots, depending on sea conditions and loading, the bow foil generates sufficient lift to raise a substantial part of the lower hull clear of the water, thus reducing frictional drag due to the viscosity of the water and providing a 'sprint' speed of 40–45 knots.

At the time of writing, about thirty craft of this type were in service. A series production programme is underway, involving more than one yard in Western Russia and one in the Soviet Far East. Production is estimated at between four and five units per year.

Power Plant: Three 5,000 shp ChNSP Type 56 16/17 diesels, each driving its own propeller shaft.
Hull: Welded steel structure based on that of the Osa missile-craft.
Armament: Four 21 in. single AS torpedo tubes, a forward 25 mm. twin-mount and a twin automatic 57 mm. AA mount aft.
Electronics: Surveillance radar, Pot Drum; fire-control radar, Drum Tilt, IFF, High Pole antenna and Square Head radar.
Dimensions: Length 39.3 m. (128 ft 11 in.): beam 25.1 m. (82 ft): draught 1.8 m. (5 ft 11 in.)
Displacement: Standard displacement 200 tons, fully loaded 230 tons.
Performance: Maximum speed foilborne, 40–45 knots.

54 **Type 143**, German Federal Republic.
Designed to replace the earlier Jaguar class torpedo-boats, Type 143 began to enter service in November 1975. In the event of hostilities between East and West, the primary mission of the West German Navy would be to protect NATO's northern flank in the Central European Sector, and to counter any attacks by the Warsaw Pact navies in the

approaches to the Baltic. In order to fulfil these tasks the craft would be responsible for attacking enemy surface forces, landing forces and logistics units; protecting NATO minelayers and also protecting themselves against attack by aircraft and missiles.

A feature of Type 143 is the installation of a fully integrated command and fire-control system (AGIS) comprising radar, computer, display units, data transmission and a fire-control system. The radar provides surface and air surveillance, target identification, weapons direction and tactical navigation. A data transfer system permits direct automatic information exchange with other surface vessels, aircraft and land bases, enabling the flotilla commander to obtain target assignment instructions.

Originally it had been intended that boats of this class should carry SM-1A Tartar missiles but this concept was disregarded in favour of the MM 38 Exocet when tests showed that the latter, a surface skimming missile, could not be diverted by hostile counter-measures even when radar had picked up the oncoming missile.

Keel laying of the first took place at Lürssen Werft, Bremen-Vegesack in April 1972. Since then a further six have been built at the same yard. Three others were built by Krögerwerft, Rendsburg. Total cost of the ten craft, including development, has been reported as DM 760 million (U.S. $270 million).

Power Plant: Four MTU 16V956 16-cylinder V-type diesels, each developing 4,000 hp maximum continuous and 4,500 hp cruising. Each engine drives a three-bladed, fixed-pitch propeller via a reverse and reduction gearbox.

Hull: Composite transverse-framed construction. Frames, bulkheads and deck beam of welded construction in light alloy. Longitudinals, deck beams and machinery platform in welded steel. Triple thickness, diagonally bonded wooden outer skin bolted to alloy ribs.

Complement/Accommodation: Forty officers and men. Living

and working quarters fully air-conditioned. Full protection provided against NBC attacks.
Armament: Four launchers for Exocet MM 38 missiles, two Oto Melara 76 mm. guns, one forward, one aft. Two 21 in. Seal wire-guided torpedoes aft.
Dimensions: Length overall 57 mm. (200 ft): beam 7.8 m. (24.6 ft): draught 2.8 m. (9.5 ft).
Weights: Nominal displacement 295 tons, fully loaded 378 tons.
Performance: Maximum speed, calm conditions, 38 knots.
Range: 1,300 n. miles at 30 knots.

55 **Type 148**, German Federal Republic.
With the introduction of the Soviet Komar and Osa missile-craft in the 1960s, it became obvious that, in the event of hostilities, the West German Navy would be incapable of countering attacks on the approaches to the Baltic with its Jaguar torpedo-boats. At the time, the only anti-ship missile available in the West was the Exocet MM 38, and the only fast patrol boat equipped to launch it was the then new Combattante II, itself a derivative of the German-designed Saar-class, built in France by Constructions Mécaniques de Normandie (CMN) of Cherbourg. CMN added 2 m. to the design for the Israeli craft to provide room for four Exocets amidships. With no obvious alternative in sight twenty of these craft were, therefore, ordered by the German Federal Republic in October 1970 and were commissioned between October 1972 and August 1975. Hulls for eight were built by Lürssen, but all were returned to Cherbourg for fitting out. In a similar manner to the Schnellbooten of World War II, Type 148 vessels are numbered S-41 to S-60.

Power Plant: Four MTU MD872 lightweight marine diesels, each delivering 3,600 bhp and each driving a variable-pitch propeller via a reverse gearbox.

Hull: Steel.
Complement: Four officers and twenty-six men.
Armament: Four MM38 Exocet launchers amidships, one 76 mm. Oto Melara rapid-fire dual-purpose cannon forward and one 40 mm. Bofors gun aft. Eight mines can be carried aft with the Bofors 40/70 gun removed.
Fire Control System: Vega-Pollux; Thomson CSF Pollux radar.
Dimensions: Length: 47 m. (154.2 ft): beam 7.10 m. (23.29 ft): draught 2.50 m. (8.20 ft).
Weights: Standard displacement 234 tons, fully loaded displacement 265 tons.
Performance: Max. speed, 39 knots, cruising speed, 35.5 knots, range, 600 miles at 30 knots.

56 **Willemoes**, Denmark.

Modelled on Sweden's highly successful Spica class torpedo-gunboats, the 240-ton Willemoes class was designed to the requirements of the Danish Navy by Lürssen Werft. Construction, however, is being undertaken by the Frederikshavn Vaerft and Flydeclok which was contracted for a ten-ship series.

A CODAG propulsion system is employed with three Rolls-Royce marine Proteus gas-turbines for sprint performance, and twin GM V71 diesels on wing shafts for cruising.

Pennant Nos/Class Names/Years of Commissioning:
P540 Bille (1977); P541 Bredal (1977); P542 Hammer (1977); P543 Huitfelde (1977); P544 Krieger (1977); P545 Norby (1977); P546 Rodsteen (1978); P547 Sehested (1978); P548 Suenson (1978); P549 Willemoes (1976).
Power Plant: Three Rolls-Royce Marine Proteus gas-turbines with twin General Motors GM V71 diesels on wing shafts for cruising.
Hull: Steel construction. Rounded bilge hull form.

Armament: Torpedoes/missiles: Four 21 in. torpedo tubes, the after pair of which are due to be replaced by Harpoon missiles. One 76 mm. Oto Melara 76/62 dual-purpose gun on the foredeck.
Electronics: Torpedoes controlled by a Philips Elektronikidustrier PEAB TORCI 204 and dual-purpose gun and missile by a Philips 9LV 200 fire-control system.
Crew: 6 officers and 18 ratings.
Dimensions: Length overall 46 m. (151 ft); beam 7.4 m. (24 ft); draught 8 m. (2.4 ft).
Displacement: Fully loaded 260 tons.
Performance: Maximum speed 38–40 knots.

57 **Wisla**, Poland.

Few details of this 70-ton fast attack torpedo craft have been published. It appears to have been designed as a replacement for the ageing P.6s transferred to Poland by the Soviet Navy. Production began in Poland in the early 1970s and at least fifteen are currently in service.

Power Plant: Lightweight marine diesels.
Armament: Four 533 mm. (21 in.) torpedo tubes, two each side of the superstructure, and one fully automatic twin 30 mm. AA mounting of Soviet design.
Dimensions: Length overall 25 m. (82 ft): beam 5.5 m. (18 ft): draught 1.8 m. (6 ft).
Displacement: Loaded weight 70 tons.
Performance: Maximum continuous speed 30 knots.

58 **Vosper Thornycroft 52 m. Fast Missile Boat**, United Kingdom.

A highly automated missile craft designed for service into the 1980s, this striking new 52 m. design is the biggest patrol boat class built so far by Vosper Thornycroft. Armed with four Otomat missile launchers, an Oto Melara 76/62 compact gun and a Breda 40 L/70 twin naval mounting, it has a maximum speed of 40 knots.

A derivative of the Company's highly successful Tenacity class, which has been employed by the Royal Navy for fishery protection duties in the North Sea, this new generation missile boat is fitted with roll damping fins and has particularly good sea keeping characteristics powered by four 4,000 hp. marine diesels; it has accommodation for forty officers and ratings.

Power Plant: Four Paxman Valenta 18 RP 200M marine diesels, each with a sprint rating of 4,000 hp. at 1,600 rpm and a maximum continuous rating of 3,500 hp at 1,500 rpm. Each drives a fixed-pitch propeller via a reverse/reduction gear box.
Hull: Round bilge hull in welded mild steel.
Superstructure and Weather Deck: In sea water resistant aluminium alloy. Divided into eight watertight compartments.
Complement Accommodation: Crew forty. Air-conditioning in living compartments, operation room, radio room, enclosed bridge, gun bays/magazines and machinery control room.
Armament: four Otomat anti-ship missile launchers; one Oto Melara 76/62 compact gun with 300 rounds of ammunition; one Breda 40 L/70 twin naval mounting Type A, with stowage of 736 rounds on gun and magazine stowage for a further 720 rounds.
Electronics: Marconi S 810 band stabilized MTI Surveillance radar; Decca TM 1226 'I' band Navigation radar; Decca RDL–2ABC passive EW system; one MEL Protean chaff launching system.
Fire Control and Action Information System: This includes a Marconi ST 802 I-band tracking radar; a CCTV system with autotracking unit; optical fire directors with laser range finder; Sperry digital directors to enable the 76 mm. and 40

mm. mountings to be controlled against air and surface targets and the Otomat missile fire control system.
Dimensions: Length overall 52 m. (170 ft 7 ins); moulded beam 7.6 m. (24 ft 11 ins); draft over propellers, 2.45 m. (8 ft).
Performance: Maximum speed 40 knots; maximum continuous speed 36 knots.
Range: 1,900 n. miles at 15 knots.

59 Zobel (Type 142), German Federal Republic.

Ten of the West German Navy's Type 140–141 Jaguar class torpedo-boats have been reconditioned and re-equipped with the Seal wire-guided torpedo, a product of AEG-Telefunken. These vessels are known as the Zobel class. The Seal torpedo is fired by compressed air and employs electric propulsion. All the data required to guide it to its target is fed to its guidance system by manual or computer control from the attacking craft, or by a self-homing system mounted in the torpedo itself. Neither the launching nor the guidance stages are affected in any way by craft motion. The Seal's propulsion system provides a considerable range which allows it to be launched well outside the target defence area.

Power Plant: Four 3,000 bhp MTU 16V 538 diesels, each driving a fixed-pitch propeller.
Hull: As for Jaguar class.
Complement: Thirty-nine officers and men.
Armament: Two single Bofors L70 40 mm. cannon, plus two 21 in. tubes for Seal torpedoes.
Fire-Control System: NV Hollandse Signaalapparaten M20 series compact combat system. Dual radar system provides surface warning, tracking and air target tracking. One air target and three sea targets can be tracked automatically at the same time. Provides for the control of two guns of light or medium calibre against one air and one surface target simultaneously or two torpedoes against two targets simultaneously.

Dimensions: Length overall 42.5 m. (139.4 ft): beam 7.2 m. (23.4 ft): draught 2.4 m. (7.9 ft).
Weights: Displacement fully loaded 225 tons.
Performance: 40 knots.

60, 61, 62 Trident, Hai Dau and WS 82 Naval Surface Weapon System

63, 64, 65 Variants of the Lürssen 57 m. FPB hull.

As shown on the following three pages it it not unusual for a proven basic hull to be employed for several classes of fast patrol and attack craft. Patrol boats range from craft that rank as little more than large motorboats with limited armament to very powerful and sophisticated craft which bristle with the latest weapons and electronics. The differences in installed power and armament are dictated by the customer's operating requirements. Speed and striking power may take precedence in some cases while in others long range or simplicity of design and operating are the primary needs.

The three craft depicted are all based on Lürssen's 57 m. round bilge FPB hull.

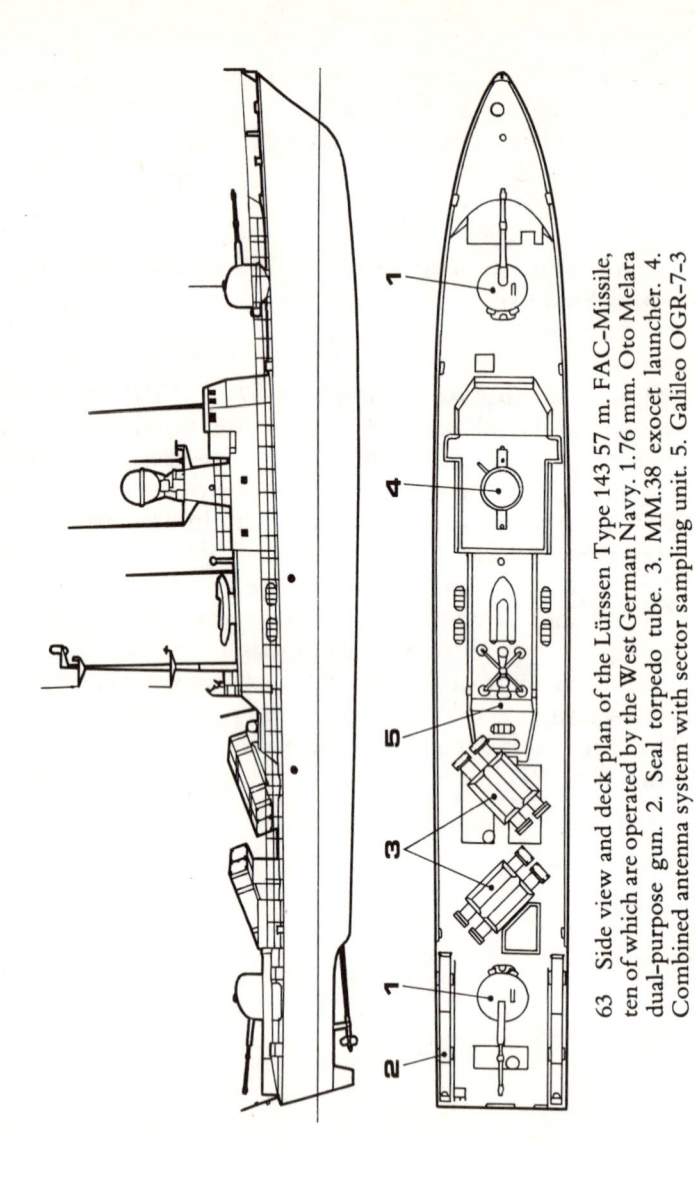

63 Side view and deck plan of the Lürssen Type 143 57 m. FAC-Missile, ten of which are operated by the West German Navy. 1.76 mm. Oto Melara dual-purpose gun. 2. Seal torpedo tube. 3. MM.38 exocet launcher. 4. Combined antenna system with sector sampling unit. 5. Galileo OGR-7-3 optical director.

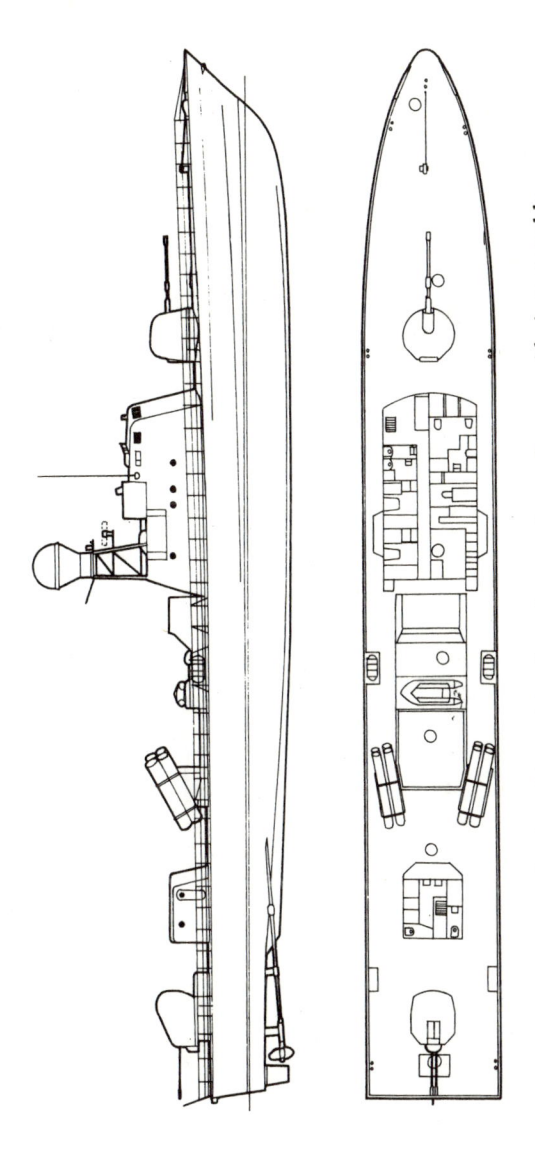

64 Turkey's offshore islands and rugged coastline provide innumerable natural hiding places for its many attack craft of which the Dogan, based on Lürssen's 57 m. hull is the latest. The Dogan, built at Vegesack was followed by the three units of this class, each built in Turkey by the Taskaisak yard, Istanbul.

173

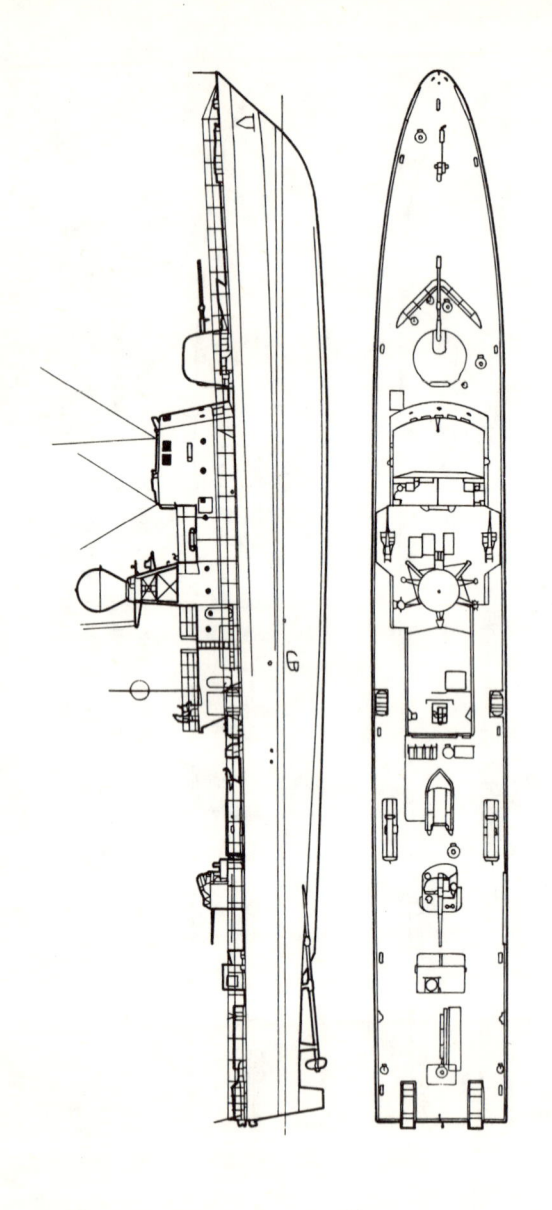

65 Side view and deck plan of the Lazaga class Fast Attack Craft-Patrol, six of which are in service with the Spanish navy. The hull is identical to that of the Lürssen 57 m. design on which the Type 143 and Dogan are based. One basic difference is the use of two MTU engines with two screws and two shafts instead of the four MTU engines with four screws and four shafts employed on the Type 143 and Dogan.

INDEX

Index to plate descriptions and plate captions. Plates are referred to in bold type.

ACM(H) 138–140
Al Fulk **2**, 99
Asheville **1**, 97
Astrapi **3**, 100
Azteca **4**, 101

BH.7 Mk 5A Wellington **5**, 102
Babochka **6**, 104
Badek (Kris Class) **21**

CPIC **7**, 105
Combattante I 106–109
Combattante II **8**, 106–109
Combattante III **8**, 106–109
Constitución Class **9**, 110–111

Dabur (Hornet) **10**, 111–112
Dogan 173
Douglas, PG100 (Asheville Class) **1**

Exocet **55**, 103, 104, 106, 107, 115, 153, 155, 157, 158, 165, 166

Federacion, P12 (Constitución Class) **9**

Flagstaff II **12**, 114–115
Freccia **13**, 116

Gabriel **35**, 115, 144, 146, 147, 150
Guacolda **14**, 116–117

Hai Dau **61**
Harpoon (McDonnell Douglas) 103, 108, 115, 123, 139–140, 144, 168
Hauk **15**, 117–118
Hu Chwan (White Swan) **16**, 118–119
Hugin (P151) **17**, 119–120

Isku **19**, 122

Jaguar **18**, 120–122
Jaguar II & III 122
Jamhuri (Madaraka Class) **2**

Kartal **20**, 123
Komar (Mosquito) **22**, 124–125
Kris **21**, 123–124

Lance **25**, 127–128
Lazaga 174

Lürssen 57m FPB Hull 172
Lürssen Type 171

Madaraka Class **2**
Mol **23**, 125–126

Nanushka **24**, 126–127
Nasty **11**, 112-114

Osa I & II **26**, 130–132
Otomat (Oto Melara) **9**, 111, 153, 155

P-6 Class **27**
PB Mk I 133–134
PB Mk III **28**, 133–134
PHM Class **32**
Paek Ku (Seagull) **29**, 134–136
Pchela (Bee) **30**, 136–137
Pegasus, USS (PHM Class) **32**
Penguin **42**, 115, 117, 118, 120, 152, 159, 160
Perkasa **31**, 137–138
Plejad **33**, 140–141

Rade Koncar (Type 211) **34**, 141–142
Reshef (Flash) **35**, 142–145

SA-N-4 148
SS-12M (Aérospatiale) **31**, 137, 138, 160, 161
SS-N-2 127, 132
SS-N-2B 142
SS-N-9 127, 148
Saar I, II & III **36**, 145–147

Sarancha **37**, 147–148
Scimitar **38**
Sea Killer 116, 153, 155, 162
Sea Wolf **39**, 149–150
Shanghai I-IV **40**, 150–151
Shershen **41**, 151
Snögg **42**, 151–152
Søløven **43**, 152–153
Sparviero **44**, 153–155
Spear **25**, 130
Spica I 155–157
Spica II **47**, 155–157
Spica M **46**, 157–158
Spica T121 **45**
Stenka **48**, 158–159
Storm **49**, 159–160
Styx 131, 132, 146
Susa **50**, 160–161
Sword **25**, 128–129

Tenacity **51**, 161–162
Tjeld **52**, 163
Tracker **25**, 129–130
Trident **60**
Turya **53**, 163–164
Type 143 **54**, 164–166, 172
Type 148 **55**, 166–167
Type 211 141–142

Vosper 52M Fast Missile Boat **58**, 168–169

Willermoes **56**, 167–168
Wisla **57**, 168

Zobel (Type 142) **59**, 170–171